Thirty As F***

30 Things I Learned During My Quarter-Life Crisis

Sarah Ordo

Thirty As F***

Copyright © 2019 Sarah Ordo

Cover Art © Caroline Teagle

https://caroline-teagle.squarespace.com

Cover Photo by Collective Image Photography

www.collectiveimagephotography.com

Edited by Cara Lockwood

edit-my-novel.com

ISBN: 9781729449981

CONTENTS

"And the beauty of a woman, with passing years only grows."

-Audrey Hepburn

INTRO

I'm starting this book at the age of twenty-nine, which is pretty damn close to being thirty. Turning thirty can be such a weird jumble of emotions. On one hand, you're getting older. On the other hand, you've still got SO much more life left. Like I said, 30 is super f*cking weird. I have had so many mixed emotions about my turning 30 in the last few years of my 20s that I figured I should just write a damn book about it...So that's exactly what I'm doing. Sharing all of the absurd thoughts, the emotional breakdowns, the life-shattering realizations, the truth bombs, the heartbreaks, and the WHAT THE F*CK moments that really shook things up and opened my eyes before the big 3-0.

You really can't entirely blame those women out there in the world who try to resist aging with everything they've got in their power. These ladies resist wrinkles, new decades, and telling people their actual age like it's the freakin' plague. In a way, can you really blame them? EVERYTHING in our society tells us to stay young. We are fed the idea that youth equals unwavering power and beauty. Just take a look at any of the Housewives and the amount of Botox and fillers in their face and it's pretty clear, we've categorized aging as an evil. We'd rather inject our face with something that literally paralyzes our facial muscles then get another frown line. No wonder we have such a fear of another year passing

Now don't get me wrong, I'm not saying that I'll never test out some Botox or fillers one day, but one flip of the channel to your favorite reality show or one swipe of your Instagram feed and it's all breast implants, lip injections, and girls barely old enough to drink with their thong bathing suit-clad *sses plastered all over your iPhone screen. Youthfulness and perfection is thrown in your face constantly, no matter where you turn.

For most of my twenties, I dreaded turning thirty. Thirty was this big looming end-point of my youth in my mind. It's like being exiled to Haiti for women like me who are in their twenties. Thirty just caused a tidal wave of anxiety inside of me. Thirty meant that I should already be married. Thirty meant that I should already be having children. Thirty meant that I should know whether I should turn the air on hot or cold in my car to de-fog the windows properly. Thirty meant that I should have already had all my sh*t figured out, right?

Seriously, most of us sit around as little girls daydreaming about how at thirty we will be married to a successful, tall, dark, and handsome man (in a perfectly tailored suit, of course), pulling a perfectly executed dinner out of the oven with our apron on. Some organic, gluten free, homemade bullsh*t recipe we found on f*cking Pinterest as a stay at home mom with all the time in the world on our hands. We imagine ourselves having this big, beautiful house with gigantic flowers planted around our white wrap-around porch where we will drink our morning coffee. We picture ourselves calling the kids inside for dinner from swinging on the swings with the dog out back, because we ALWAYS eat dinner as a family at the table in these daydreams.

Hey, um…Reality check. That's not how it's going for most of us at all.

Cut to my mid-to-late twenties. I found myself single, switching careers, and struggling to find myself again while entering into a new life of sobriety. I was losing friends that I thought would be by my side as bridesmaids at the altar when I had my picture perfect wedding day. I felt like my family was let down and ashamed by my alcohol issue. I could tell that some people thought I was absolutely INSANE to be ending my career as a preschool teacher to start my own hair and makeup company. And I was constantly asking myself WHY I couldn't find a decent man in the world when everyone else was?

There were many times that I felt like I was walking smack-dab into a quarter-life crisis. My therapist could confirm that I had many of these "quarter-life crisis meltdowns" while sitting on her brown plaid couch in her office. I was all over the f*cking place at the end of my twenties.

But I do have to admit that as my twenties came closer to an end, things started to shift. Then they shifted big time. I started to grow up. I started to mature. I started to realize that a lot of the things I had placed so much value and importance on for most of my young adult life REALLY didn't mean as much as I thought they did. The closer to my thirties I got, I really started to take on this, "I REALLY DON'T GIVE A SH*T" mentality towards a lot of things that I used to let consume my thoughts and worries.

Let me tell you, girl, it's pretty freeing and amazing to get to this point. All of you twenty-something year olds out there should seriously try not giving a sh*t about the not so important stuff sooner. It would save you a lot of ugly crying, a lot of stressing out, and a lot of empty pints of Halo Top ice cream.

I have written and created FOUR self-published works before thirty, which still is hard for me to believe sometimes. Nonetheless, writing has become a huge part of my life now. To be completely honest, I was TERRIFIED when I released my first book, *Sober as F****. If you read my second book, *Innerbloom*, then you know that I had a full-blown meltdown and anxiety attack the day I released my first book. I was receiving SO much support, so much encouragement, and so much praise for putting out my first book and sharing every raw, honest detail of how and why I got sober. Everyone had my back. Meanwhile, I was crying hysterically in my bedroom, pacing wildly, and second guessing if I really should have put so much of myself out into the world for everyone to judge.

Cue my quarter-life crisis brain to trigger me into thinking, "WHO am I to be writing books!?" I also questioned, "Maybe I'm not even old enough to be an actual good author yet." That feeling still occasionally gets triggered in me when I see the not-so-nice Amazon reviews that some people leave on my books, but I've learned that you've just got to roll with it. You're not always going to be everyone's favorite and someone is always not going to like what you do. That's life.

At some point before thirty, I eventually grew into the mindset that I don't give a f*ck who doesn't like me, who doesn't like the fact that I swear like a sailor, or who judges my writing skills. I don't write for the woman who is sitting at home pounding away on her keyboard about how she couldn't even finish half of my book because it was "written so poorly..." I write for myself and I write for YOU. The woman going through exactly the same things and stages of life that I'm going through right now.

After writing so many heavy, emotionally-charged works about my struggles and successes in sobriety, my almost-thirty mindset told me, "I want to write something FUN." I wanted to write something light, humorous, and satirical that every woman out there of any age could relate to. I wanted to write something that took something that gets such a bad rap (like turning thirty), and turn it into something we can poke fun at, laugh about, and make it into something that doesn't make us want to cry at all times. Because we have enough crying with every episode of *This Is Us* that comes out already. Seriously, I know many of you out there bawled your eyes out and contemplated never buying a slow cooker again after that one episode...don't even lie.

So I decided to write this book right before ending another decade of my life. This book essentially became the hilarious yet oddly profound journal of my late twenties...AKA my quarter-life crisis.

I've realized that this time in my life has been one where I've learned more than ever before about myself. I've learned some life lessons that I will carry with me to the grave. I'm talking life-changing, truth bomb realizations that I never saw coming. I'm talking growth as a person that you couldn't pay for or be taught in a textbook. Real life experiences and growth. The kind of things that really change you as a person. The things that will shape and form you into a seasoned, experienced, cultured, knowledgeable human being that's been around the block a few times and come back with the war stories to prove it.

I've really grown into my own self as I come in hot on the big 3-0. I've learned to love even the things I considered to be flawed about myself. I learned how to own the f*ck out of the thirty years I've had on this earth so far. And it's been one of the most empowering times of my life. I feel more powerful, more secure, more full of life than I ever have. I feel truly more confident in myself than ever before. It's indescribable at times how I've morphed from this insecure, confused young adult into this grown *ss woman who is now a force to be reckoned with.

I'm sharing all of this with you guys. My tribe. My girl gang. My circle of supporters who have had my back and supported me more than my own family and friends have at times. As I pound on the keyboard and type out book baby number five, it just feels good. It feels on track. It feels meaningful. It just feels right.

Most of all it feels like a blessing and a gift. A gift that I get to do this. I get to share all of the hilarious, crazy, life changing, f*cked up stories about my young adult life for other women to enjoy. For other women to learn from. For other women to laugh. For other women to cry. For other women to get the chills and goosebumps of reading something that makes them say, "OMG this is totally me" or "I needed this," over and over again.

This is my personal journal of all of the things I learned during the first thirty years of this amazing life. Some of them are quite humorous and a lot of them are quite emotional. Some of them involve some really heavy sh*t. Some of them might have you cracking up at the irony, because you have thought the exact same irrational, hilarious things at some point during your own young adult life, too.

We're gonna talk about cellulite. We're gonna talk about how to find love that is good and true and PURE. We're gonna talk about how your family can drive you absolutely out of your mind. We're gonna talk about letting sh*tty people go. We're gonna talk about stretch marks and lash extensions and owning everything about who you are. We're gonna cover the light stuff, the heavy stuff, and the everything-in-between stuff. Girl, we've got a LOT to cover. Thirty years is a whole lot of stuff to whittle down into one little book, but I'll do my best for ya'll.

These are the thirty things I've learned before turning thirty years old that I want to share with all of you. Whether you're eighteen years old, turning thirty, or eighty years old, I have a feeling that all of you will connect with the things I'm going to talk about in this book. These are all valuable and powerful life lessons that we all need to listen up and pay attention to. There is a whole lot of other sh*t to learn still in life, but these are my top thirty at thirty years old.

I also am going to do my damn best to show you all the things that thirty CAN be. Thirty is not mom jeans, Tupperware, and the end of all of your fun. Thirty can be anything you want it to be and whatever you choose to make it. Thirty has turned out to be the most secure I've ever felt in myself, in my choices, and in my life. Thirty feels like just the beginning of so many exciting things. Is it weird to say that at this point, I am LOVING what thirty has become to me? I'm in LOVE with THIRTY. I am loving this life. I'm gonna share all of that with you ladies, too.

What I hope to give you from this collection of realizations, truth bombs, and life lessons is love, light, and grace. Love for exactly who you are. Light to get you through the inevitable rough times in your life. And grace for you to realize that this journey called life is one full of amazing and incredible growth inside and out. This life will never stop teaching you things and never stop shaping you into the beautiful and unique woman you were destined to be. Hold on for the ride.

I hope you f*cking love it. xx.

THING #1 | THE QUARTER-LIFE CRISIS IS A VERY REAL THING

So, why the big "crisis" about turning thirty? Well, I think it all depends on how you're looking at it. We, as women, tend to overanalyze, overthink, and go a little overboard when we ponder anything related to aging when we are young. We act like aging is the plague and the devil on Earth coming to end us. Seriously, have you seen a 29-year-old's anti-aging skincare routine lately? I'm over here drinking collagen, coating my skin with a variety of acids, and voluntarily rolling needles all over my face on a regular basis in hopes of keeping my skin looking twenty-nine forever. It sounds like someone being tortured into confessing to a violent murder from a movie plot, but nope, it's just my nighttime skincare routine.

The big truth here is that aging is inevitable. We can't slow it down, delay it, or stop it for the most part. I mean, Joan Rivers (RIP to that fabulous, glamorous woman) did a pretty good job of making sure that her face delayed the aging process as much as humanly possible, but on the inside she still was getting older just like the rest of us as time passed. At some point we just have to accept the fact read my other books or followed my story at all, you are probably well aware of this. In my mind the party was never going to end for me. I still had YEARS to keep squeezing into my whore-ish little outfits and high heels every weekend. The party and the free shots at the bar were going to be my weekend agenda for a long, long time to come.

Things like responsibilities, 5-year plans, and financial security were the last thing on my mind as I was ordering Crunchwraps from Taco Bell at 4 am in whoever's car I convinced to come pick me up via drunk text messages at closing time. There was always that "oh sh*t" moment every once in a while, where life sent a little slap in the face wakeup call in the form of an epic f*ck up, a reckless drunk night, or a panicked fifteen minutes in the bathroom sitting in silence to see if one line or two showed up on a cheap, drugstore brand pregnancy test that sat on the counter next to the missed birth control pills. But, overall I was not concerned in the least bit about how far off my thirties were. The end of this party was nowhere in sight, and I couldn't have been happier about it at the time.

After I got sober and the end of my twenties started coming in real hot, I did start to shift a bit. There was a time period where I fell into the quarter-life crisis mind frame that I was almost thirty, I had no serious relationship, no engagement ring on my finger, I was still renting my townhouse apartment, and I had no babies that I had brought into this world yet. I knew that I wanted all of these things in life, and I never thought I'd be so close to thirty without accomplishing any of them yet. Cue the emotional crisis, the ugly crying, and the complete and total breakdown in front of my therapist, Debbie.

I can even remember breaking down into tears once in Debbie's office when I tried to get approved for my first mortgage while newly single at the age of twenty-eight. As I wiped the tears away that were streaming down my face, I literally choked out the words, "I just didn't think I'd be this age and doing this *alone*." The word alone was accompanied by what left like a knot twisting and tightening in my stomach. I had fixated on this idea that by the time I turned thirty things would have fallen into place for me in all areas of my life.

I thought that at the age of thirty I would have met an amazing man that I would share buying my first home with. I thought I'd be planning my wedding already. I thought maybe I'd turn thirty with a little baby on my hip. But on that day in my therapist's office, none of those things had happened for me yet, and I was finally accepting the fact that the daydream I had always played in my head as a young girl wasn't going to pan out exactly how I always thought it would, when I thought it would.

When I was younger, I had created this picture in my head of how my young adult life would play out. I think a lot of us do this as young girls. We sit and we play with our dolls in our dollhouse. We play a game of "House" where Mommy and Daddy live together in their white picket-fenced home with their shiny new car. Daddy is grilling in the backyard and Mommy is setting the picnic table for the family. Daddy has a great job that provides for the whole family, and Mommy takes care of the children and may also have an amazing career as well. The children are happy and playing games while laughing in our perfectly mowed backyard.

There are no money-triggered fights between Mommy and Daddy. Daddy isn't sleeping with the doll at work on the side. Mommy isn't self-conscious about her boobs that are now saggy from breastfeeding. Daddy doesn't spend weekend nights too drunk to drive home at the local dive bar. Mommy isn't trying to scrap together the money to simply feed the children everyday. Daddy isn't taking Mommy to court over child support and visitation schedules. Mommy doesn't cry herself to sleep every night. Daddy doesn't raise his voice and break things when he's angry. Not in my perfect dollhouse world.

I would sit on my carpeted bedroom floor for HOURS playing with plastic dolls that recreated this perfect life scenario I created. Many of us do this as little girls and our perfect little naive storyline we've created with our dolls is the one we will carry over into our young adult lives. It's no wonder that we start to panic and have a bit of a "crisis" in our lives when our perfect storyline that we created as a young child doesn't play out before our own eyes.

Why do I not have that handsome man grilling in the backyard yet? Why am I drowning in student loan debt and shopping the clearance racks religiously? Why am I renting a one-bedroom apartment and not buying my first white-picket fenced home with my husband? Why did the first man I truly loved lie and break my heart with his cheating? And WHY aren't my breasts perfectly shaped and perky just like my Malibu Barbie that drives the pink convertible with her heart-shaped sunglasses on?

Our perfect little storyline from playing with our dollhouses and daydreaming about our lives falls apart and we realize that life is going to be very different than we daydreamed it would be as young girls. Crisis.

Another reason for our "crisis" is the idea of time. Do we have enough of it? Are we wasting it? Can we please have some more of it? As women, many of us think that we never have enough time in the day. We try to get as much as humanly possible done in the time that we have. We set high standards and create big dreams for our time. We often joke about needing more than 24 hours in the day. If we could get that 25th hour, you know we would savagely grab it and try to get even more done with it if we could.

Time is a funny idea to focus on. It is not a concrete thing, we cannot hold it in our hands, and we cannot control it. It's an elusive thing that never stops. One thing that the idea of time causes us to do is to worry about what we are doing in relation to it. Are we using it wisely? Are we accomplishing enough during it? And women, as you probably know ALL too well, love to plan according to it. We love being organized, knowing exactly what's going on, and creating timelines for ourselves and for others. That's just what we do.

We create timelines of when we think things should happen in our lives. Some of us more than others, but a LOT of us women do this. Haven't you ever overheard a group of girlfriends talking about when someone's boyfriend or girlfriend is going to pop the question? "It's about time!" is often the response we hear that a woman has been dating someone for a long period of time without a ring on her finger yet. As soon as you do get married, it immediately shifts to "When are you gonna start having babies!?"

There is the general practice happening of always immediately jumping to the next thing that we think should be happening. Why? Because we create timelines for our lives. We believe that after a certain amount of time, a proposal should happen. We believe that after a certain amount of time being married, children should be happening. Timelines, timelines, and more timelines—all because of this idea of time.

The reality of the whole thing is, that the timelines we create for ourselves aren't real. We've invented them out of thin air and they technically don't really exist. They're the fairy tales we tell ourselves, and those stories don't always come true when we think they should. Cue the crisis.

I was SO bad about doing this. I basically had created a checklist and a timeline for my young adult life that essentially was not real and did not exist. I convinced myself that by thirty I should have been starting all of these things in my life. I had put these big red stamps on my life about when I should have been married by, when I should have had children by, etc. Why? Because I'm a woman and sometimes we get super hard on ourselves and give ourselves these unrealistic pictures for our lives and how we think they should be by a certain point in time. Because we are having a damn quarter-life crisis again, per usual.

Come on, ladies, I think we can all admit that we've done this before. We are so hard on ourselves and put so much pressure on ourselves to meet certain expectations in life, whether they are our own or someone else's. That's exactly what I was doing for way too long. I was feeling like I had done something wrong because what I thought should have been happening by the age of thirty wasn't happening for me yet.

I was being a bit ridiculous, and I can see that now looking back. There was nothing wrong with me because these things simply hadn't happened yet. There was no reason for me to be in crisis. But at the time, the panic was ALL too real.

I will say this…the closer I get to turning thirty, the more I'm fine with the fact that I don't have all of those things yet. Why? First, because I don't FEEL thirty at all. I don't feel "old" or like I am running out of time in the least bit. I can still run miles during a workout to balance out the large pizza I ate the night before, I can still rock a pair of heels like a pro, and I'm nowhere near being a hunched-over, wrinkly old woman any time soon when it comes to my appearance. I've definitely got the starting of some fine lines and dark spots, but I've had people tell me "You don't look anywhere near thirty!" and you know that I not-so-secretly am LIVING for those comments. But seriously, I don't feel old in the least bit. If anything I'm realizing just how much I'm capable of doing and being still. I feel like I am in my prime right now if anything!

The second reason why I'm fine with being behind on my once-created, non-existent "timeline" I created for myself is that I'm able to acknowledge and appreciate all of the things I HAVE accomplished so far in my life.

I may not have a wedding and kids under my belt yet, but I've got some huge accomplishments, amazing travels, and incredible life experiences under my belt instead. Seriously, this will be my fifth self-published piece of work I will have completed by the time I turn thirty, which is still so unreal to me. I launched and produced a podcast all by myself when I had absolutely no freaking clue how to do any of it. I own and run a successful, award-winning on-location hair and makeup company in the Detroit area. I've started doing Mindset Coaching via an app on my phone for multiple women at a time. I have lived on my own and paid all of my own bills for YEARS. I've traveled alone to amazing places. I've even been featured on national television for God's sake! I have done SO much before even turning thirty. When I lay it all out like this, it's easier for me to be like, "Clearly you're doing fine, psycho. Now take it down a notch."

I think it is so crucial to shift our mindsets to this place of acknowledging what we do have and what we have done rather than what we are lacking or have not done. It really helps to chill out the crisis vibes quite a bit. We need to chill those the f*ck out.

The crisis just is not necessary. It's a very, very real thing, but at the other end of it I have a feeling you will be laughing thinking back on how much you stressed about a day that in reality, is just another day. Because guess what? One day you're gonna wake up to turning forty. After that you're gonna wake up one day to being sixty. And one day you just might wake up to be a cute little ninety-three-year-old grandma with so much love and life in your soul that you will feel plain old blessed for the years you've gotten to live. So let's chill out a bit with the crisis, because thirty is really just the beginning of this beautiful life we get to live.

THING #2 | 30 IS NOT "OLD"

Let's get one thing straight right from the get go...30 IS NOT "OLD." I learned this one real quick as my thirtieth birthday came rounding in on me. It might sound a little old when you are young, but if you really think about it you still have a LOT of time to live your life well beyond thirty. People live longer now than they ever have in history, so thirty is really just the beginning. You could literally live to be one hundred years old. ONE HUNDRED YEARS OLD. Wrap your head around that one while you're over here worried about little old thirty. When you think about all of the menopause, hot flashes, saggy skin, gray hair, and senior citizen discounts that await you in your future, you've got plenty of time to get it right still.

Some of the most exciting times of your life will probably come after you pass the big 3-0. I don't know about you, but the fact that one day I'll reach menopause and no longer steadily bleed and not die every 28 days is enough for me to be a little bit excited about the things that will come in my future years. I could go on and on for PAGES about this, but I've got an entire book to do exactly that. Don't worry we'll be covering ALL of the exciting things that have yet to come in our lives after hitting thirty years of age.

I dare you to stand in front of someone from the baby boomer generation and tell them that you are SO old. Better yet, try standing in front of someone that is in their late eighties pushing a walker around in front of themselves in a retirement home and tell them that you are SO old. Betty is gonna want to straight up hit you upside your pretty, not-yet-fully-gray head with her walker if cute little thirty-year-old you tries to tell a woman that has raised four children and nine grandchildren that YOU feel old over here about to turn thirty years old. Brace yourself.

I think it really puts it into perspective when you talk to someone that has more years on you. I've found myself many times rambling on and on about how "I'm getting so old…" in front of people that are much older than I am. At some point I realize by the look on their faces that I sound like an idiot to be b*tching and whining about getting old to someone that is actually much older than I am. They are probably looking at me thinking I've lost my damn mind. They're probably looking at my barely there wrinkles and fairly perky boobs wanting to laugh in my face about my throwing around the word "old" so casually.

Think about it this way, one day you and I will both be that fifty-something woman raising teenagers, balancing a career, and trying to keep her damn man in one piece on a regular basis. We will be rolling down the windows of our car to cool down from the hot flash that just hit us while we pick up a carry out for dinner because we forgot to take the chicken out of the freezer to thaw for dinner. We will be extinguishing fights between siblings about who gets to watch their shows on the big TV when Dad already has taken it over for Monday Night Football. We will be coming home to start a new anti-aging serum that is supposed to turn back time for our weathered skin. As we finally get to kick back and breathe for the first time that day after wrestling out of our control top shapewear we sweat through during our massive hot flash…Imagine a little thirty-year-old, fresh-faced young woman complaining to you about how "old" she is at that moment. You'd be seeing me during visiting hours at the local county jail following that one.

Okay, so I'm totally exaggerating, but you get where I'm going here. When you really think about our age compared to a huge majority of the people in the world, we are not old at all yet. We are really just in our prime with SO many things still waiting for us in life. And to be honest, we sound silly even saying all this crap about how old we are out loud.

A phrase that I noticed I have thrown around often in my twenties is that I don't want to be an "old mom." First of all, what does that even mean!? Janet Jackson just had a baby at like fifty years old, so I think it's time I stop throwing around the "old mom" thing so casually. If Miss Jackson literally just pushed a human being out during her fifties and is doing fine, I have absolutely no room to talk about doing it twenty years younger than she did. But I think it's normal for us to think this way about becoming a mom because of our biological ticking time clocks we tend to obsess about. Is it just me or does the volume of that clock try to get louder and louder with every year that passes?

I've even done that thing where you sit around and think, "Okay, if I had a baby at thirty, then I'd be forty-eight when they graduate high school. I'd be fifty with a teenager...holy sh*t, will I even make it to grandkids!?" Then, of course, you have to follow that up by figuring out exactly how old you could possibly be when they get married and grand babies could come into the picture. Because we, as women, need to know everything in advance so we can mentally prepare ourselves as best as we possibly can (or at least think that it's possible to do that). Checklists, timelines, and menopausal hormones, ...oh my.

I know you've done it too, so don't act like I'm the only woman out here overthinking way too many things in life when it comes to my years. We all do it. In reality, I was being absolutely insane to say that being thirty makes me an "old mom." It's even been proven by doctors that your early thirties are a woman's optimal time to have children as far as her health and body are concerned. I definitely let out a little sigh of relief when I heard that study come out. See, these ovaries really are just getting ripe and we are in our prime, ladies!

Staying with the "old mom" topic, I have worried from time to time that if I get too old or wait too long that I might struggle to have children. I hear so many heartbreaking stories about women suffering multiple miscarriages, struggling with infertility, and so many other emotionally and mentally draining things while trying to have children. Sometimes I can't help but feel a little rushed to have my own because of all of the things that can go wrong. But I always try to remind myself that if it is meant to happen for me it will happen for me, exactly when it should. Sometimes I've just got to reality check myself to keep my mind from wandering too far on the topic.

A common theme I'm noticing here is that I was overthinking WAY too many things about my age. I was fueling the fire to my own quarter-life crisis by fixating on the idea that I was getting "old." I was holding a massive can of gasoline over my head and dousing myself to really get the fire that was my quarter-life crisis blazing by thinking this way. But as many of us have learned in life, you are what you think and what you surround yourself with. If I continuously focused on the negative things, the worries, and continued to overthink EVERYTHING about my age, of course it was only going to amplify every thought, concern, and worry I had about turning thirty. I had to reel it in and get my sh*t under control. I had to get my mind in a better place about this time in my life.

When we look at history, men and women used to typically be married and having children by the time they turned thirty. It wasn't unusual for a young woman to have already been in a serious relationship, already planned and been through her (first) wedding, and welcomed her first child into the world all by thirty years of age. But things today are very different for young women.

For some people, getting married young and having children may still be the way they foresee their life going, which is TOTALLY fine.

Some women and men are bound to be settled into a little family and a lifestyle like this way before thirty even comes near. I'm not hating on it, because there are times I wish I had those things already a little bit. But, it's also 2018, we have birth control that can be implanted into our arm that lasts half a decade, and a WOMAN just ran for president for the first time in history...So clearly things have changed a little bit and we have way more possibilities for our lives as a woman today than just being a wife and wearing mom jeans at thirty.

Maybe we're at that weird awkward stage of adjusting to how the times have changed and how we have changed. Remember when you had your awkward stage around puberty? Your boobs started growing, you had to start shaving places you never had to shave before, and you were kind of becoming a young woman while still in a baby fat-cushioned body? You didn't know if you were ready to be a young woman, but you kind of had to start being one. You got to the age where it just happened, and we all know that we can't stop time or go backwards in life.

I feel like that's where we're at when it comes to the quarter-life crisis. We're ready to be adults and take on anything that life throws at us, but we're still trying to hold onto our youth and our life full of never-ending possibilities too. We're literally back in the place where we got our first bra and started shaving our legs with raspberry scented shaving cream all over again. Except this time, we're trying to excel in the world as a strong and successful adult woman whose got it all together. We're doing that while also wanting our freedom, our opportunities to do whatever we want, and our pre-dark spot covered complexions to just remain forever young. It can be a bit of a tug of war, really, because it's another big time of transition in our lives.

Here's the thing. This time is NOT at all about being "old" and we should definitely NOT be treating it like we're counting down our days left here on Earth. We've got plenty of time left. Plenty of time to make big changes. Plenty of time to make big mistakes. Plenty of time to figure it all out. Plenty of time to continue to live our lives.

We are NOT old at thirty years of age. This is a time of transition.

This is a time of transformation. This is a time of being a strong, powerful woman that lives a beautiful life. It's a point where we are appreciating but maybe growing beyond our wild, carefree millennial dream-filled twenties. But it's also a time to realize that we still have so much more to do and see and live. To realize just how much more we are capable of doing still in life.

This is a time when we should be truly living in the idea of "30 is the new 20." Okay, so I've always thought that phrase was a little bit ridiculous. I feel like people just take whatever age they are and insert it into the blank of "_____ is the new 20" just to make themselves feel better. Like, I'm not about to bedazzle it onto a frame and hang it up in my bathroom for a daily morning reminder of eternal youth. But seriously, it IS kind of true…

We are at a place in time where thirty has NO limits. Thirty CAN be the new twenty. It is still a clean slate, a fresh start, and an unwritten life. It is a point in life where we still have SO much time left! Nobody is telling us we have to do one thing and not do another. Nobody has written out directions on a road map that starts at the age of thirty for us. We have the opportunity to still do absolutely WHATEVER we want in life. To be honest, we have that same opportunity whether we are thirty or eighty-seven years old. There is nothing stopping you from what you want to do, see, and accomplish in life at any age, thirty included.

I know you've all seen those posts about how Oprah got fired from a news station, J.K. Rowling was a single mom living off of welfare, and Tina Fey was working at a local YMCA all during their twenties. They didn't even figure their sh*t out yet by thirty. I know some people might roll their eyes at all of those posts, but this one truly hits the nail right on the head. There is no point in life where you should be feeling old and like life is over, because there is no point in life where you cannot flip the script and rewrite it all… especially if you're only thirty years old. You are just in your prime, baby girl.

Rather than looking at thirty as being old and a death sentence to our fleeting youth, let's look at it as a new decade where things can really take off for your life. It's another year to chase after your dreams. It's another year to fall in love with your soulmate. It's another year to travel and see the world. It's another year to have your first child (or your fifth). It's another year to do whatever the hell you decide you want to do in your beautiful life.

Thirty is just another year to be anything but "OLD" and we have got to drill that idea into our heads. It's like that line from *13 Going On 30* that Jennifer Garner repeats over and over again with her scrunchie-clad side ponytail while she is hiding in the closet wishing she was thirty years old. "I want to be thirty, flirty, and thriving…" she repeats over and over again, "THIRTY, FLIRTY, AND THRIVING." I mean, if a thirteen-year-old teenage girl can grasp the idea that thirty isn't "old," then we should be just fine being able to do the same.

THING #3 | THERE'S NO RIGHT WAY TO BE "ADULTING"

I love how often we see #adulting all over Instagram plastered on photos of millennials doing everyday tasks like cooking a meal, doing laundry, or attempting to get their sh*t together. Basically, everyday tasks for most people out there in the world. But seriously, what the hell does "adulting" even mean!? Just to be a little bit extra, I googled it for you. Here's what Urban Dictionary says:

Adulting (v): to carry out one or more of the duties and responsibilities expected of fully developed individuals (paying off that credit card debt, settling beef without blasting social media, etc). Exclusively used by those who adult less than 50% of the time.[1]

I'm literally laughing out loud at the part that says, "Exclusively used by those who adult less than 50% of the time." First of all, let me point out that this is Urban Dictionary's definition of what adulting is, not good ol' Webster's. I honestly don't even think this word is in the actual dictionary at this point in time, but hey...never say never. There may be a day you turn to the A's in your dictionary and there it will be as a verb in all of its ridiculous glory.

So "adulting" can be summed up in my own definition as essentially doing things that a proper functioning human being adult person is capable of performing to be responsible. It seems easy enough. By "adulting," we should be able to pay our bills, clean our place up, be financially responsible, and act like a somewhat mature individual in society. It probably means that we shouldn't be acting like Ramen Noodles cooked in the microwave are a nutritious "meal" after the age of twenty-seven. It probably also means that we should know not to throw that one red sock in with our load of whites in the laundry load. But let's just bust this whole adulting idea down real quick…

My initial question when I hear the word adulting is how do you know that you are officially an "adult?" At what point in time do you get a big red stamp across your forehead in life that brands you as an adult? Seriously, when does this happen? If you wanna try to go by age, we could say it happens at age eighteen, twenty-one, thirty?

I don't think there's any age that on that day of your celebration of birth everything changes and you have evolved into a new class of human being known as an "adult." I don't think there is any specific number of years you have to have on this Earth to qualify you for the elusive adult title. There's no magic number where it's just going to happen and you will wake up one day thinking, "Oooooh, I'm an adult now!"

If you want to look at gaining more responsibilities as making you into an adult, I think it's a struggle to try to actually create any logical timeline. There are women that become mothers at the age of sixteen that are the farthest things from "adults" I've ever seen (thanks, MTV). There are women in their thirties out there that can't keep a job. There are grandmothers out there in their freakin' sixties and seventies that have done terrible, irresponsible things and landed themselves in the slammer. I mean, have you watched any of the Netflix documentaries where a grown a** woman is absolutely crazy and accused of plotting an insane murder!? The point I want to make here is that you can be handed years of life experience, multiple children to take care of, and a lot of work to be responsible to complete and that in no way, shape, or form means that you are an "adult" in my eyes.

Does gaining more rights and freedoms make you an adult? You can buy cigarettes and vote for the next president at age eighteen, and you can order a dirty martini in the United States at the age of twenty-one…Does that make you an adult? Don't think so. The same young women buying cigarettes at a gas station and heading over the border into Canada to legally drink at age nineteen can be the same girl fighting with her mom about why she can't stay the night in a dirty Days Inn motel every weekend with her "friends" because she's "an adult now." P.S. if you didn't already figure it out, that was TOTALLY me living in denial at age nineteen when I thought that I knew everything in life and was trying to argue with my mom that I was an adult. I think we can all agree that I learned that those things were definitely not true rather quickly.

It seems that there is no checklist you can complete to officially achieve the label of "adult" in life. There is no set timeline, no certain destination, and no specific qualifications for being considered an "adult." There is no specific moment in your lifetime where you are going to feel some crazy wave of adult-ness come over you like you're being tasered by life that will transform you into this super-charged, has-all-the-answers-now human being from that moment forward. It's just not going to happen.

So what we must understand about "adulting" is that there is no right way to be an adult. There is no certain age where it automatically happens. There is no tour guide taking us through how it works. Nobody is pointing out to us each little thing that we should be doing. There is no instruction manual made for us to read before navigating the journey of our lives. There is no GPS or App on your phone that's giving you real-time directions. It would probably be a whole lot easier for a lot of people if there was something out there to tell us exactly how it works, but it just does not exist. We're totally on our own with this one, ladies.

So what does "adulting" look like to me at this point in life? It looks like a lot of things. It looks like keeping your place clean. It looks like not calling your mommy anytime something goes wrong. It's being able to take in your own car for an oil change. It's keeping food in your house to cook actual meals. It's knowing how you should and shouldn't act in a variety of situations. It's knowing that the bad boy is not the right choice. It's being smarter with your money and actually having a savings account. It's being able to stand on your own two feet and make decisions for YOURSELF. It's all the things.

I'm about to turn thirty and there's times where I still feel like I'm trying to figure this adult sh*t out. There are times I ask myself, "What in the actual f*ck AM I doing?" There are literally situations that happen every day where I am going on Google to find out, "How long do hard-boiled eggs last in the refrigerator?" or, "Where can you buy stamps?" Don't even laugh about the stamp thing. A few months ago I literally posted a Facebook status asking everyone on my friend list where you can buy stamps besides the Post Office. Go ahead and laugh, but I literally had no idea what the answer to that one was.

Just about every week something happens that makes me question my adult-ness. Not as far as age is concerned, but more related to my knowledge or skills or the things I've acquired in life. Does it make me less of an adult that I just now bought my first home with my almost fiancé? Does it make me less of an adult that sometimes I still wear my pajamas until 1pm while working from home as I turn thirty? Does my still DVRing every episode of Teen Mom make me less of an adult? I just really, really love watching the girls try to figure their sh*t out. And I personally love watching Chelsea and Cole make weird baby voices at each other and be so disgustingly cute that I just want to squeeze them to death and be their best friends.

At this point in my life I find myself wondering if I haven't figured out all the stuff about how to be adult yet, will I ever? Will I ever actually feel like I've arrived to that magical place called being an adult? I definitely feel like I already qualify as an adult now, but there's still things I'm figuring out every day! Will that change at forty? Fifty-seven? Eighty-two? Will I ever have that "AH-HA!" moment where I figure it all out? Probably not.

I think what I've realized is that this thing called life is always full of twists, turns, and surprises. Just when you think you've got being an adult figured out…BOOM, you get audited by the IRS for your taxes being screwed up. Just when I think I've got this budgeting thing figured out financially…BAM, you've gotta dig into your savings to redo the driveway that's cracking apart. Just when you think you find the "right" guy or girl… SURPRISE, they were being a phony putting on a performance the entire time. Just when you think you're getting it all under your belt, something new will always come into play. Plot twists. Life changes. New jobs. Surprise pregnancies. All the things. Because that's just life.

Here's the thing about this idea of being an adult. It's all about the journey. It's all about the growth. It's all about constantly learning new things about life and about yourself as a person. There's no start and no end. It's not a real thing you can see or touch. It's not a concrete thing or an actual object. It's an idea. It's a word. It's a way to classify, describe, or even judge people of all ages.

I've been guilty of using the petty phrase, "Act like a f*cking ADULT," during a fight or two in my day. It's a great low blow when you're accusing someone else of doing the wrong thing. It's a way to try to hit it where it really hurts and make them question everything about where they are at in life. Was it my finest hour when I used this sentence as a hurtful comeback during an argument? Absolutely not. But did it hurt the feelings of the other person when I accused them of NOT having their sh*t together and not being an actual adult? ABSO-F*CK-ING-LUTE-LY.

We don't like people to tell us that we are doing things wrong. We don't like to be criticized in a way that makes us question ourselves and who we are. I mean really, who wants to be told that they are doing life itself wrong after being over a certain number of years old? Not many people are going to like that accusation. They get downright angry and defensive at the very suggestion of it. It makes them feel less than. It makes them feel immature. It makes them feel like a child. It's makes them feel like you're telling them that they just aren't doing good enough in life. Ouch.

Here's the truth bomb. The bottom line. The thing I've realized myself as I get closer to thirty by the day... Nobody can really give you a clean cut definition of what being an adult (or "adulting") really, actually means. It's everyone else's ideas and opinions of what it means that create the idea of it in their own head. It's subject to outside influences like what we've experienced in life, what's important to us, and what others have told us is right or wrong.

You may have created this idea of what being an adult means from your own opinions or from your parents' opinions that they took on as they grew up. You may have created your definition of what being an adult is by the things you have seen or experienced in life. You may have been taught that certain things equal adult-ness by a teacher or a mentor. But really, nobody has any f*cking clue of what being an adult actually means because there is no REAL definition or guideline for it. It's all just a big combination of ideas, personal opinions, and characteristics that seem appropriate for people beyond a certain age.

Being an adult for you might mean being a mom. Being an adult for her might mean being able to afford and pay all of her own bills. Being an adult for him might be learning how to cook for the kids when Mom goes back to school for night classes to get her degree. Being an adult for you might have been stepping up to help keep the family on track while a parent struggled with an addiction of some sort. Being an adult for you might have been when you left your first emotionally abusive relationship. It's individual to each and every person out there and it is unique to their own journey in life.

Do you see what I'm getting at here? Being an adult can be

different for every single person from every single walk of life. It can mean one thing to one person, and something very different to another person. Being an adult can start at one point for her, and a very different point for you. There might be days for the rest of your life where you don't feel like you're "adulting" through certain situations.

There's no real answer to this question of when we become an adult. It's individualized for all of us. It'd different to all of us. When I realized this truth I also realized that I should just stop trying to figure it out once and for all. Stop worrying about what it meant and if I was doing it right. Stop trying to figure out all of the details about it. Stop feeling bad if I didn't know how to do certain things at this age. Accept the idea that throughout my life there's always going to be moments that I might not feel like I've mastered it all yet, and that is absolutely fine.

The realest truth I learned about "adulting" and becoming an adult? You've got to just live your life doing the best you can, doing the things that make you truly happy, and doing whatever it is that works for you at that point in time in your life. Sure, you can be open to striving to really nail this being an adult thing, but try not to sweat it too much. Don't worry about what others say and know that you've just got to live in your truth and nobody else's, regardless of what age you are. Live in a way that makes YOU feel like you're doing just fine when it comes to "adulting," and don't worry about the rest.

[1] Urban Dictionary (2016). https://www.urbandictionary.com/define.php?term=Adulting

THING #4 | YOU'RE ALLOWED TO GIVE YOURSELF A BREAK

I am the QUEEN of overworking myself. I've got a crown on top of my head with glimmering, sparkling diamonds and jewels when it comes to putting WAY too much on my plate to the point of having a complete meltdown from time to time. I'm talking ugly-crying, mascara-running, straight-up emotional tornado breakdown. It's not pretty and it is definitely not my finest hour, but for some reason I got stuck in the cycle of piling way too much on my plate, trying to do it all, and then falling apart over and over again. I'm not sure why it took so long for me to realize that that wasn't normal, but I finally got the point y'all.

I've always felt the need to do EVERYTHING, and to do it as perfectly as I possibly can. I've done it from a very young age so it's an extremely hard habit for me to break. I'm definitely not that little girl anymore who would cry and be late for third grade because she had bumps in her ponytail and HAD to redo it until it was perfect. I'm getting better at it, which is what we're going to chat about in this chapter, but that took a whole lot of change and growth within myself.

I'll be the first to admit that it wasn't easy to change this habit, and I still feel it resurface from time to time. But the point is that I've made major progress. At one point, telling me to give myself a break would have been like telling Kylie Jenner to stop having her lips done. It just wasn't gonna happen. No way. No how. Never in a million years. Sorry, wrong number. That voicemail mailbox is full. Try again later.

Seriously, when I was twenty-two years old, I was in Cosmetology school full time, taking night classes to teach Early Childhood Education at the University of Michigan, working as a receptionist at a hair salon, go-go dancing at nightclub in Detroit on the weekends, and also doing hair on the side at home for my friends and family (for nowhere near enough money, I might add). Did I leave that poor twenty-two-year-old girl enough time to even breathe?

THIS is what I've always done, and I've realized now over time that it was never necessary to live this way. It was never necessary for me to work myself to the point of hysteria several times a year on the calendar.

Some of you may be able to relate to WHY I always felt the need to do this. I never thought about the reasoning behind why I always did this to myself. Why did I cram so much on my plate that I literally ended up in tears at least once every couple months, having a complete and total meltdown? Why did I pull all-nighters before every exam in college and then go to work immediately after and drink three extra-large coffees to keep myself going when I felt completely and totally exhausted? Why couldn't I just pick one career and one path for schooling? Why did I insist on working at a nightclub until 4 a.m. every weekend when all I really wanted to do was take a night off? Why was I SO hard on myself and why couldn't I just cut myself a f*cking break!?

I came to the conclusion of why I did this for the first time in therapy after getting sober. My therapist and I came to the conclusion that I was extremely uncomfortable being by myself or alone. We discovered that by working on things constantly, I kept myself distracted from the things about myself or my life that I did not want to face or deal with at the time. I also came to the personal realization that I believed that if I was being successful in my career it was my own f*cked up way of convincing myself that I hadn't lost all control yet with my drinking.

How could I have a problem with alcohol if I was excelling in so many things in the work sector of my life? "See, girl, you're not an alcoholic! Look at all of the stuff you're doing..." was something I was telling myself in my head the entire time. Can we say DENIAL? I was refusing to acknowledge my issue with alcohol, and convincing myself that my success couldn't possibly allow that to be true was my way of masking it. So I continued to pile as much onto myself as I possibly could to keep that facade going.

As women, we have a terrible habit of putting way too much on our plate. We think we are superwoman and that we can handle any and every little thing that life throws at us all at once. Not only do we think we can do this, we think we *have* to do this. And we have to do it all PERFECTLY.

Now don't get me wrong, we ALL want to feel like superwoman. We all want to feel like there is nothing that we can't do. But we get this idea in our head that we have to do EVERYTHING and that we have to do it all to absolute perfection. We get stuck in this place where we just keep loading more and more onto our backs to carry. It's just so much unnecessary pressure and stress, and the worst part and reality is that WE are the ones that are putting most of it on ourselves.

I recently read the book *Girl, Wash Your Face* by Rachel Hollis and found myself almost in tears when she explained how and why she did this exact same thing in her own life. It hit home with me so hard that I couldn't help but get emotional as I read her words. I sat there thinking "OMG... this is ME" as she described how she felt like she constantly needed to be accomplishing or creating something to feel "good enough." She went on to describe how she never even celebrated the things she accomplished as she completed them, because she was already throwing herself into her next project by the time the previous one was finished.

THIS is EXACTLY what I had done with my first three self-published books. THIS is EXACTLY what I did when I launched my own website. THIS is EXACTLY what I did when I created my podcast. I never cut myself a break. I never celebrated any of my accomplishments as much as they deserved to be celebrated. I was too busy already moving onto the next thing before I could even stop and pat myself on the back for my latest accomplishment. It made me realize that how I had been pushing myself was so very wrong.

I got quite emotional when I realized that both myself and Rachel Hollis were repeating this horrible habit without realizing it for a long, long time. We gave ourselves credit for nothing because we were too busy fixating on what else we could accomplish and what we could do next that was bigger and better.

I realized in that moment that I had barely acknowledged the launch of my third self-published book, *Sober as F***: The Workbook*, because I had already thrown myself into writing this book. I should have been SO FREAKING PROUD of myself for launching not one, not two, but THREE self-published books all on my own in less than a freakin' year! Instead, I was throwing myself into this book because someone had left an Amazon review of *Sober As F**** saying they, "...couldn't even get through half of it," because it was, "written so poorly..." My response was to obsessively write my next book because it would be better and that would give me some sort of reassurance that I was doing something well. Maybe if I wrote another book, a better book, it would make that bad review go away in my head, right?

I posted an Instastory bragging about how my third book hadn't even launched yet and I already had my first three thousand words written in this book that same day. Why? Because I needed to do something to make that negative review go away. Because I let someone with an Amazon username about unicorns who had probably never written anything longer than a three-page paper about World War I in high school convince me that I was a bad writer. I allowed someone that didn't even have an avatar photo make me feel like I wasn't doing good enough in life. WHAT IN THE ACTUAL F*CK?

I've also got to make a point here about the current trend of women using words like "hustle" and "grind" all across social media to describe their work ethic. First of all, YES, I've been guilty of using these words in my own posts. Not too long ago, I was all about showing the world how busy I was on social media and plastering #HUSTLE in the caption to really show everyone that I was working hard and killing it out here.

The more I've realize how crucial it is to give yourself a damn break, the more I've began to despise those words now. We use words like "hustle" and "grind" to describe our work ethic all the time. We use them to show the world how we're killing it out here as women in the working world. We're making it on our own. We're paving our own path in life. We want everyone to think that we are enough and that we are doing enough. And we're gonna hashtag every damn word we can think of to describe how hard we're working to convey that to you on our Instagram feed. Not healthy.

So let me reel it back in here. I realized that I was working myself crazy for pretty much all of my twenties. I realized that I was piling way too much on my plate constantly. I realized that when I was single, throwing myself into being a #FemaleEntrepreneur pounding away on a laptop until 1am every night was the norm for me. Because #HUSTLE, right?

What I learned was that I needed to start giving myself a f*cking break. To be honest, I resisted it like hell at first. I was so used to being this strong, independent woman who was accomplishing all kinds of crazy awesome things in my career. The thought of not working as hard as I had been for pretty much all of my life felt like an American trying to drink the water in Mexico…not a good idea, a huge mistake, and possibly going to make me s*it my pants at some point out of pure fear. I thought it was going to ruin my career. I thought I was going to lose everything I had worked so hard to build in my life. I was absolutely terrified and more than uncomfortable about the idea of taking a break.

My therapist would ask me every week during our sessions, "So... how late were you on your laptop in bed this week?" to see if I was making any changes or progress. It took a long time for me to able to honestly tell her that I wasn't still on my laptop past midnight every single night. It took baby steps. You know how babies are when they are learning to walk: they stumble, they fall, and for a while they just can't get it no matter what they do. Well, that was me trying to make myself relax and give myself time off.

Telling an overachiever to take a break sounds like you're speaking a language to them that they don't understand. Someone telling me to give myself a break felt like someone was standing in front of me rambling out words in Spanish, while your girl only knows as much Spanish as Justin Bieber sings in the song "Despacito."

I think that getting into a relationship was the thing that ultimately pushed me into forcing myself to take time off. But, guess what? I fell head over heels in love with it. I began to LOVE getting all my work done in the morning so that I could make a cup of mid-day jasmine green tea with honey and watch a few episodes of some trashy girly show on Netflix. I became over the moon excited about planning little vacations and getaways where I wouldn't be working at all. I freaking ADORED giving myself a time to cut off work to get ready for a date night of dinner and a movie with my boyfriend. I learned to look forward to quiet days at home in comfy clothes with no makeup on...LIKE, WHO WAS THIS NEW CHICK!?

Giving myself a break and time to relax and recharge was not ruining my life. It wasn't setting me back in my career. My business wasn't crumbling to the ground because I stopped double booking myself. My books were still selling whether I worked sixteen hours a day or six. Recording just one podcast episode a week didn't stop women from listening to it. Life was still going on, I was still building my career, and SHOCKER, the world continued to spin on its axis even if I took a day off for myself.

So here's what I learned: learning how to give yourself a break is not only okay, but it is totally necessary. Like you need oxygen to breathe kind of necessary. It is so crucial to our health, to our well-being, and to our entire quality of life. It keeps us from having those meltdowns on a regular basis. It keeps us happy. It keeps us healthy. Just do it. And do it often.

Taking breaks gives us time for US. We need that time to take care of ourselves. We need time to make sure that we are good to go. We need to make sure we give ourselves enough rest. We need to make sure we give ourselves enough time to relax and recharge. We need to make sure that we are mentally sane. We need to make certain that we are doing everything we need to do to assure that we are at one hundred percent in our own lives. We need to give ourselves the damn break we need sometimes. We need to be able to do all of these things. If we don't take a break to take care of ourselves, how can we show up for all of the people and all of the other things in our life at one hundred percent?

Learning to cut ourselves a little slack and give ourselves a break needs to be a part of life. Try to think of it this way: if we make sure that we are our absolute best, taken care of selves, then we can be that person in everything that we do. We can show up as the absolute best version of ourselves for every person, place, and thing in our lives. We can be fully present and fully taken care of emotionally, mentally, and physically. It's a win-win situation for everyone really. But mostly for ourselves, because that's who needs to practice better self care as a way of life.

I have a feeling that so many of the women reading this are guilty of being exactly like I used to be. You are probably juggling a career, a family, a household, and five hundred other things on a regular basis. You probably feel like it's ALL on your shoulders, ALL the time. And if you're around my age or older, then you may just relate to my feeling that we're just f*cking tired sometimes. We're not eighteen years old anymore doing it all on no sleep and a diet of drive-thru tacos. We are at a point in life where we need that break. We need it and we just f*cking deserve it. Period.

THING #5 | IT'S OKAY TO SAY, "NO"

Let me be honest about something here…I HATE being out late. I love spending an entire evening at home wearing my comfiest sweatpants or leggings. I love being wrapped up in warm, fuzzy blankets with a hot cup of ginger lemon tea with honey in my hands. I love being in bed before eleven o' clock on a Saturday night watching old seasons of *Hart of Dixie* with Rachel Bilson with my Chihuahua, Kaya. I LOVE waking up around 7 am on the weekends to read my Bible and write on my laptop. You might be thinking, "Okay Grandma, do you also love to have an ice cold glass of prune juice while watching *Murder She Wrote* reruns regularly?" while you're reading this. Check back with me when I write *Forty As F****, I just might be there.

Sometimes I feel like the most boring, geriatric twenty-nine-year-old in the world when I see Instagram posts of girls my age that are out in L.A. at the hottest clubs, in the tightest-fitting dresses, wearing the highest of high heels…But then I think about spending a Friday night in eating copious amounts of Jets deep dish pizza and turbo cheese bread (and LOTS of Ranch) with Andrew with absolutely no makeup on, watching episodes of *Naked and Afraid*...and then I don't feel so bad. That sounds like absolute HEAVEN to me.

The point I want to make here is that I am a complete and total homebody now. I don't drink anymore, I don't like going out super late (except for certain special occasions), and I don't enjoy being at a bar or a nightclub every weekend. A few years ago I would have been in that tight-fitting dress, I would have been dancing at that nightclub, and I would have been wearing those highest of high heels next to my old girlfriends.

Oh, I would have been THAT girl, for sure. Falling all over the place on a liquor-coated concrete bar floor, flirting with any guy at the bar with his wallet out, and convincing my girlfriends that we couldn't possibly pass up that rager of an after-hours party in an old warehouse. Why? Because I felt like I had to. I felt like I had to go out, I had to have "fun" and I had to be that wild party girl to be happy. To be seen as popular. To possibly meet a man. To make others think I was enough. To make myself think that I was enough.

I HAD to say YES to everything. I couldn't possibly be missing out. I couldn't possibly let the FOMO ("fear of missing out") seep in. I had to say YES. I had to make others think I was living the most fun life EVER.

This was right up there as one of the biggest bullsh*t lies I have ever convinced myself of. That I had to say YES to everything whether I wanted to do it or not because I felt like I HAD to. Because I felt like what others might think if I was to stand up and say NO was going to be a terrible thing. If I said no and missed out on something, what would I possibly do with myself? And also, if I said no and it pissed someone else off, how could I possibly do that!?

Well, sobriety, growing up, and becoming a somewhat adult changed that attitude of mine a whole lot. Now, I say HELL NO to the things that I do not want to do ALL the time. And you know what? It feels f*cking AMAZING.

When I learned that I could say NO to the things I did not want to do, I felt like my entire life changed. I was back in the driver's seat and I was in control of whatever the hell I wanted to do. When I realized that I had every damn right to say NO to the things that did not serve me or add to my life in a positive way it was like WATCH OUT, WORLD!

NO, I don't want to go to that party. NO, I can't stay at work an hour later today. NO, I don't want to post an Instagram photo talking about your product that I don't actually use or even like. And NO, I REALLY don't want to join your online LulaRoe party. Twenty-four dollars for a pair of leggings with cartoon dogs all over them is really not on the top of my list of things I want to invest my money in at this point in my life. And I also don't want to receive notifications every seven minutes on Facebook that you're having a live sale. Trust me, if I change my mind about the cartoon dog leggings at any point, I will be sure let YOU know right away, Karen.

We have absolutely no obligation to say yes to the things that we do not want to do. Obviously, there is going to be a grey area where there are some things you can't say no to. These things can include feeding your children, filing your taxes, and doing your own laundry because your husband doesn't know how not to shrink every shirt in your closet. But those things don't apply to what we are talking about here. I'm talking about the things that you are not gun-to-your-head or legally obligated to do.

I'm talking about the extras. The invitations. The things you feel pressured or forced into doing. The places you feel you have to make an appearance at. The favor you feel like you have to do, knowing it will never be returned. The things that serve you no f*cking purpose AT ALL. The extra things and the optional things.

I heard something about this in a standup comedy special on Netflix recently, and the comedian made a joke about how amazing it feels to cancel plans. Of course I laughed along with it, but guys, he was SO freaking right.

Something about deciding that I didn't want to go to my ten-year high school reunion in the basement of a bar we all congregated at every weekend over a decade ago felt amazing. I made the decision for myself, and not for anyone else. When I decided that there was nothing about paying a cover charge that didn't cover drinks, food, or get me ANYTHING for that matter that was appealing to me at all, I felt great. When I thought about why I would attend a reunion where everyone I used to party with would be smashed drunk before 10 p.m. while I was coming up on my three-year anniversary of sobriety...I couldn't think of many good reasons to say yes. So I decided to just say, "No, thank you." Nothing there appealed to me, so I chose to say no. Decision made. Zero guilt. End of story.

I know some of you would never miss your high school reunion for anything in the world. But the point I want to put the spotlight on here is that when I found myself looking for reasons to convince myself to go...I knew that there was no point in going. There was nothing making me actually want to go. I wasn't looking forward to it. I was actually struggling with deciding on whether to go or not for WEEKS. That amount of internal conflict you experience about doing something speaks volumes. It didn't serve me. It didn't add anything positive to my life. I also wouldn't die if I didn't go because I have been following all of these people on Facebook since graduation. Because I felt like I was convincing myself to do something I didn't really want to do, I said, "NO." LOUD. AND. PROUD.

If something doesn't feel right and you don't really feel like doing it, then don't do it. It sounds simple enough, right? Well it absolutely can be! Like I said earlier, unless it's something that you are absolutely obligated to do (or legally obligated to do), you have every right to say "NO" to anything that doesn't feel right, positive, or good to you for any reason whatsoever. You don't even need to explain yourself or your decision to anyone unless you somehow feel the need to.

Think about a toddler when they are first learning how to talk. "NO" is their response to just about everything once they learn that powerful two letter word. But you know what is awesome about that? They feel absolutely no shame, no regret, and no guilt for using the sh*t out of it. They literally say no to EVERYTHING with zero hesitation.

NO to the cereal puffs. NO to the diaper change. NO to the nap. NO to the oversized bows velcroed into their baby hairs. That two letter word is spoken, yelled, screamed, and cried through snotty tears with zero hesitation. No second guessing. No wondering if they might be hurting someone's feelings. Just a selfish as f*ck "NO" shouted from the rooftops. I mean come on, isn't the thought of it kind of exhilarating? Girl…BE that toddler.

Okay, so we don't have to literally act like a toddler. I don't know about you, but I'm way past that whole sh*tting my pants on a regular basis thing. But what I want you to focus on is how toddlers can say "NO" so easily without even thinking twice about it. They do not stop or hesitate for one second to think about who they might offend or piss off by saying the word no. So, why can't WE do that?

At what point did we, as adults, take on this attitude and stigma that saying no isn't okay? At what point between the toddler years and now were we brainwashed that that two letter word was the anti-Christ and the root of all things evil in the world? Two letters do not hold that much power, sister, I can promise you that.

First of all, we have choices in life. Choices are a beautiful thing and I hope you're already taking full advantage of them. We have choices and we have the freedom to make decisions for a reason, to exercise them. If we were meant to not have choices in life, then the word "no" wouldn't even exist. We would have a straight line path throughout life.

We have the right to create boundaries regarding the things we don't want or need in our lives. We have the right to choose the things we want to do and do not want to do for a reason. That reason is because it is our life to design and live. If you're not exercising that right already you really should start, like yesterday. The fact that we have choices and can carefully pick and choose the things in our lives and what we decide to do in them is amazing. It is empowering. It needs to be taken advantage of WAY more often than some of us are doing it.

It's not all just about making choices and saying no. It's about using your intuition. It's about the way you get those gut feelings sometimes about things that you simply cannot ignore. You know that feeling you get when something just doesn't sit right with you? When you feel hesitation and uneasiness in the face of it? When you feel blocked or like something just isn't flowing or happening as easily as it should?

We get those feelings for a reason. When something just doesn't feel right, that's your gut intuition telling you something. It's not only trying to tell you that something doesn't feel right, it's often screaming it to you from within your own body and mind.

Start tuning into it. A gut intuition is something that we can harness SO much power and influence from that it's insane. If you are open and accepting to feeling it, it can direct you and guide you towards and away from many things in your life. It can steer you in the direction you are truly meant to go in and make you stop dead in your tracks if you're going the wrong way. It can be a truly awakening spiritual practice in your life to start listening to it on a regular basis.

It might sound a little crazy and woo-woo to you, but start tuning into your heart, mind, body, and soul. They can absolutely speak to you. They can tell you what you need more of. They can tell you what to walk away from. They can give you so much insight if you just start listening. Start tuning in and listening to what they are trying to tell you. Feeling tired? That's your body telling you to rest. Feeling uncomfortable with that guy? That's your heart telling you it isn't going to work. Feeling emotionally drained? That's your heart telling you something in your life is pulling you down.

When I first got spiritual in my own life after getting sober, I was SO skeptical of all of the woo woo energy and "listen to your soul" type of stuff. I don't think I had ever taken one second to concentrate on what my intuition was telling me in my life back then. Maybe I would have changed my life a bit sooner if I had, but who knows. I just kept pushing and pushing myself to say yes and do more. To do everything.

Once I cleaned up my life, I had a new, much stronger connection to my body, my spirit, and my soul. I could actually FEEL when things weren't right. I could feel it within my body when something was wrong. I could feel that uneasiness in my stomach and in my heart when I was supposed to say no about something. I felt the stirring to protect myself, to redirect, and to find what felt right instead. This was when I started listening to my own body and soul when it came to saying no. It was like having a little GPS system in my gut that was notifying me to turn right in 500 feet and make a legal U-turn when possible.

If you get really comfortable with yourself spiritually, mentally, and emotionally and really start to listen and feel what your body and soul says, you can absolutely start to do this practice too. When something is stirring within you or just doesn't feel right, try to sit down and be present with it. Really be open to feeling what your body and soul are trying to tell you. Let it all in. LISTEN. FEEL.

What feels right, comfortable, and guided? What feels natural? Follow THAT. What feels blocked, uncomfortable, or wrong? Say no to THAT. This is what trusting your gut intuition feels like. And that is exactly what it's going to require from you…TRUST.

Having trust in your feelings and your decisions is the only way to banish the guilt that may arise about saying NO. Be ready because you might feel that guilt creeping in for quite some time if you're not used to making decisions like this already. It's going to feel weird. It's going to feel foreign. It's going to feel plain old WRONG to some of us when we start to shift the way we feel about saying no.

You might feel bad. You might feel selfish as f*ck. You might feel like the biggest narcissistic piece of sh*t out there living in the world today. But the reality is…you're not.

Some of us are so warped in today's world, believing that focusing on ourselves and what we need is bad. We get this weird complex about how we are being selfish if we do too much for ourselves. We feel self-centered. We actually feel bad or uneasy about it. Somewhere along the way we learned that doing what was best for us is wrong, and that we should be worrying about others first instead.

Yeah, f*ck that. Here's a truth bomb about that one…You can absolutely be kind and compassionate to others in your life and still put yourself first. There are some situations and times in our lives where it is absolutely okay and even somewhat necessary for us to be selfish like this. To ask ourselves what we need and to put ourselves first. To love ourselves first. To make sure we are taken care of and well. Doing what is best for ourselves and our well-being is one thousand percent one of those situations where it is absolutely okay to be selfish like this.

As long as you are not hurting or harming yourself or someone else, SAY NO and feel damn good about it. Feel empowered about it. Feel ALIVE for doing it. It can be a truly inspiring thing to finally stand up and say NO after feeling like you couldn't for so long. It can feel like finally breaking through the chains of whatever story you had been telling yourself about why you needed to say yes and just go along with things. It can change everything about your life.

Start listening to your mind, body, heart, and soul. Start to pay attention to what feels right and what doesn't. Start making choices for you. SAY NO. Listen to what you need. Listen to what feels right.

I can honestly say that doing this changed more in my life than I ever realized was possible. Ya'll have got to get onto this way of living too. You deserve it. You deserve the selfishness. You deserve the right to say NO. You deserve to live in a way that is totally and completely in tune with who you are, what you need, and what you want in your own life.

THING #6 | JUST GO.

I know you guys are just as guilty as me of looking at every hot girl with perfect boobs' blog about traveling. She sits in her perfect teeny tiny black bikini with her perfect long, thick ponytail, dangling her feet into the crystal clear water outside of her Maldives hut on the water without a care in the world. Then when you scroll through her other posts, you see her in the cutest outfit EVER twirling in a field in front of the Eiffel Tower in Paris. Oh, here she is on a private boat in the islands of the Bahamas with a spread of fresh fruit and a chilled bottle of champagne sitting on the front of the boat sunbathing. Hold on, are we looking at the travel destinations or the super-hot model with the bangin' body plastered all over these photos? I'm also already questioning, "HOW do these people afford to travel CONSTANTLY?"

Seriously, are these people getting flight deals or something? Because I'm over here checking my Hopper App daily to see if flights for the imaginary trip to Europe I'm not really booking are dropping this morning. I'm wondering how irresponsible it would be to just book a cruise during my slow season of work. I'm also questioning WHY it is so damn expensive for a roundtrip plane ticket to ninety percent of the places I wanna travel to...

If there is one thing that I learned I loved doing during my late twenties, it is definitely traveling. Traveling opened my eyes and brought me back to life during one of the darkest times in my life. I was in my first year of sobriety, had just been treated like absolute sh*t by the last two men I'd been involved with, and I was desperate to find something that made me feel alive and happy again. That thing ended up being traveling.

When I originally told my therapist that I wanted to travel somewhere, but none of my friends had the money or the time to go anywhere with me, she said, "SO GO..." I looked at her with a slightly puzzled look on my face. I had NEVER traveled anywhere alone at the age of twenty-six. I had done family trips when I was younger, I had done a sloppy, wasted Spring Break with friends at eighteen, and I had done an alcohol-fueled cruise out of Miami with a group of newly single girls that was an absolute sh*tshow during my mid-twenties, but nothing absolutely solo.

I realized that I had never gone anywhere by MYSELF. Completely ALONE. A million thoughts instantly ran through my head about if my life would turn into a scene from the movie *Taken* starring Liam Neilson, and that I didn't know anyone like Liam Neilson that could come save me from human trafficking. I also wondered how in God's name was I going to get my carry-on bag in the overhead compartment with my barely five-foot-tall stature when it was definitely already going to be pushing the max weight limit at the terminal check-in.

I was initially totally uncomfortable with the idea of traveling alone. It was new and exciting, but something I had never done. It was a little intimidating and scary to think about it before the trip came, and I often found myself playing out scenarios in my head that I had made up about everything that could possibly go wrong. But at the same time, it also made me feel so bad*ss and like a total boss when I told people I was going on a trip ALONE. Something about it made me feel independent and strong. It made me feel like I was experiencing more in my life. It seriously empowered me on a whole other level before I even left for the trip. It was giving me some SERIOUS *Eat, Pray, Love* vibes. It ended up turning out to be one of the most important and liberating things that I ever did in my life.

In less than six months, I went to Savannah, Georgia, Las Vegas, and California...ALL BY MYSELF. It was a HUGE deal to me. I didn't go balls-to-the-wall and do any crazy international trips alone, but those first three trips I did do within that year completely and totally by myself changed me to my core as a young woman.

Not only did I spend days completely by myself, but I had to learn how to actually be comfortable being by myself for those long amounts of time. I had to navigate airports, connecting flights, and confusing directions all on my own. I had to interact and make friends with complete strangers daily. I even had to stay at the airport overnight with a guy around my age in Atlanta when our flights got delayed and then cancelled due to weather conditions. Our bags were checked, all of the hotels in the area were booked, and we literally spent the night together watching movies on my Kindle on the floor of the Atlanta Airport. It could have been a total upset and disaster, but we laughed our *sses off while I brushed my teeth and removed my makeup in the airport bathroom. We cracked up as we ate snack bags of Chex Mix at 4 a.m. laying on the airport floor using our clothes as blankets, because it was so uncomfortable that neither one of us could actually fall sleep.

I learned so much about myself during those solo trips. I had always been a "do my own thing" kind of girl, but this took it to another level. Those trips showed me everything I was capable of doing and seeing all on my own. They showed me that I didn't need permission or anyone else to go out there and live my life. I didn't need someone with me to experience and see the world. I could go out there and see and live every little thing on my own.

Sure, I had some awkward moments, like going out to dinner by myself and feeling extremely fidgety and like I had to play with my phone because I imagined EVERYONE in that restaurant was staring at me. I was convinced that they must have all been wondering why the hell I was alone while I was eating my clam chowder in a restaurant with amazing swamp views down South. They definitely weren't, but I had convinced myself at the time that every single person in that restaurant was staring at and judging me.

I had some moments during those trips where I was alone in my hotel room early and wished that someone else was there to keep me company. Those moments brought in doubt and uncomfortable feelings. Those moments triggered some serious anxiety in me. But I pushed them out and made myself do this.

I proved to myself that I was a grown *ss woman fully capable of being on her own. I proved to myself that I didn't need someone else with me. I proved to myself that the only person holding me back from all of the experiences out there in the world waiting for me was myself.

There were some things I hesitated to do or go see while on those trips because I just felt uncomfortable at the time doing some of them by myself. But that's life. You go through and navigate uncomfortable and foreign situations. You learn that you actually can go to a restaurant by yourself and survive. You learn that you can handle cancelled flights and even make friends and have a movie night sleepover at the airport because of it. You can even meet up with a guy you matched with back home on Tinder that just happened to be in the same state for work while you were there visiting. He just might rent a car and get a hotel and you two just might spend two days exploring the islands off the coast of Georgia and driving down moss tree-lined back roads and become good friends from total strangers.

The point I want to make here is that you need to be open to the experiences in life. The places you can go. The things you can see. The new ones, the unknown ones, and the liberating ones. Don't let fear or doubt or anything else keep you from living the sh*t out of all of it.

JUST GO. Stop questioning if you should go. Stop playing out in your head every insecurity of what could go wrong. Stop saying that you shouldn't spend the money on the plane tickets. JUST. GO.

Many people might be scared off or thinking that I'm crazy for going somewhere alone, sleeping on an airport floor with someone I barely knew, or meeting up with someone I matched with back home on Tinder while on vacation. But these experiences are the ones that gave me hope again. They made me feel alive again. They became the stories I will talk about years later and laugh and smile about. I was putting myself out there to experience new places, new people, and to truly experience life and anything it chose to put in my path. I was completely open to everything traveling alone could teach me and show me.

Traveling alone *can* be a little dangerous, unfortunately. It's sad that we have to think that way as women, but it is true. Be aware of your surroundings, don't let people know where you are staying alone, and let a friend or family member know where you are and what you're doing. As long as you are careful, aware of your surroundings, and being smart, traveling alone can be one of the most empowering things you can do in your life. Just make sure you are being smart and safe while you're doing it. And get ready to be transformed as a person down to your core.

Take it from me, it truly changed me as a person in a time that I was so desperate to learn who I was again after getting sober. I had been battling cycles of depression, feeling like I'd lost everyone I knew, and I was so desperate to feel alive again. Who knew that a simple solo plane ticket held the power to change all of that for me so quickly.

When I realized that I wanted to travel more, I made it a point to promise myself a few trips each year. Whether it was by myself or not, I promised myself that if I wanted to go…I would JUST GO. I would stop second guessing it, stop worrying about the money, stop worrying about taking the time off of work. I was hungry for more experiences. I was hungry to see more of this beautiful world.

I've kept that promise to myself the past few years, and it's been one of the best things I've allowed myself to do. I get the stirring every so often that I need to JUST GO, and now I listen to it.

Thankfully, Andrew is totally on board with it most of the time. He lets me look up different places we can go, book flights, plan road trips, and search out the best local food spots to pig out at. We are the biggest travel foodies you'll ever meet. He's actually totally on board with my planning our possible future destination wedding as I finish this book that just might be on the beautiful sunny beaches of Mexico with a small group of our closest family and friends. Our love story actually began with a trip, so it only made sense to incorporate our marriage with a trip as well. That trip we took to Maine three days after meeting each other was where we fell in love and decided that this was it. I've loved so many of my vacations, but Maine was definitely the trip that stays closest to my heart and that I'll never forget.

Our first date was three days before I was set to go on this vacation solo. I had wanted to go explore the coast of Maine for basically my entire sobriety, and I had finally booked it. He joked about how he would miss me while I was gone on our second date (literally the night after our first date). I joked that, "'You should come to Maine then…"

He bought a ticket last minute (a VERY overpriced last minute ticket, I might add) and off we went. The fact that we fell in love cramped in a tiny, no-frills cabin in the woods outside of Bar Harbor, Maine just seems like it was destiny now looking back. We explored the most beautiful, rocky shorelines, ate lobster every day, and fell so deeply in love with each other within a week that it really should be the story line to the next Nicholas Sparks book and ensuing box office smash hit movie. My contact info is on the back cover, Mr. Sparks, if you need to reach me with a contract.

So if you are sitting around reading this chapter and are envious of the travels I have mentioned…JUST GO. Stop holding back. Stop worrying. Stop second guessing. Stop looking at travel bloggers on Instagram wishing that it was your life. Stop worrying about the money. Stop worrying about requesting the days off from your boss. You deserve to live and experience so many people, places, and things in your life. The world literally exists for you to go and LIVE in it. So…JUST GO!

Now let me interject here while I'm getting all kinds of fired up because I know there are things that can keep us from being able to travel. We have strict schedules, deadlines at work, children that need to be kept alive, and airplane tickets are just too f*cking expensive sometimes. My suggestion to you is to plan ahead and make it work. Arrange for Grandma and Grandpops to watch the kids for a long weekend. Budget a small part of your monthly income into a separate account for "vacation funds," and figure out the times in your work schedule that would be easiest to take a quick getaway.

I literally have made vacations and traveling a part of my budget. I make sure that I set aside a little money whenever I can so that I'm not just charging my way into debt just to travel. I make it work. I figure out what I can do to make it my reality. And side note, AirBnB is your best friend when it comes to finding reasonably priced places to stay that sometimes offer more than any overpriced hotel can.

As I'm typing this chapter right now I am actually at an AirBnB with Andrew in West Palm Beach, Florida. I'm sitting in the backyard by an in ground pool under tropical looking canopies, surrounded by palm trees, and watching baby lizards run around on the fencing. I'm working outside during the early morning hours catching a little bit of the Florida breeze before the sun gets really blazing. Sitting here with my laptop…working on this book…sipping on my morning cup of coffee with Reese's peanut butter coffee creamer…YES, PLEASE. I'm here right now doing what I'm doing because I made it happen. I planned it, I booked it, and now I'm here enjoying every second of it.

I know traveling is not something all people like to do all the time, but I do it as often as humanly possible. I make sure that every once in a while, we get these little getaways, even if they are short. We flew down here just for a quick four-day trip to celebrate my three-year sobriety anniversary. We wanted to simply float around in our private pool, drive by the jaw-dropping mansions on Ocean Ave, do a lot of relaxing, and eat delicious food together.

Not only do I think this elevates our quality of life doing these little getaways, but I think it also is so healthy for our relationship. It's so easy to get caught up in all the stress and schedules we have on a weekly basis that we don't always get to spend a ton of time together. So being able to spend quality time together for days is the cherry on top of the already amazing ice cream sundae.

What I've learned is this: don't just daydream about being able to travel. GO. It doesn't have to be super expensive. It doesn't have to be more than just a few days. Stop saying you wish you could travel more, and start traveling more. Because honestly, what are you waiting for? Money? Time? Permission? F*ck that.

If you want to travel, then just GO. You'll never regret living your life in new places, making new memories, and having new experiences. Are you ever going to seriously look back on your life when you are ninety years old laying in a hospital bed and say, "I really wish I wouldn't have spent that thousand dollars on a flight and vacation to that all-inclusive resort in Mexico on the beach that one time." I don't think so. Unless you are one of those Americans that foolishly drank the water in Mexico and got violently ill, having to hug the toilet all week, I highly doubt it. So, just GO.

THING #7 | KARMA TRUMPS REVENGE & HATERS ARE JUST A PART OF LIFE

Do you know how many times in my twenties I wanted to get revenge on someone that deliberately hurt or screwed me over? Do you know how much I wanted to get the psycho guy I met online arrested after he came to my brother's house and keyed the word "whore" into my car (spelled wrong, of course)? Do you know how much I wanted to go straight up cat fight on the girls that would talk sh*t about me behind my back in high school? Do you know how strong the urge is to take a baseball bat and bash every single light in on your ex-boyfriend's truck a la Carrie Underwood in ninety percent of her music videos after finding out he cheated on you and was concerned that the girl that knew nothing about you might be pregnant? Let's put it this way…if I would have listened to that devil on my shoulder telling me "DO IT, B*TCH!" every time I wanted to seek revenge or get back at someone, well I'd probably be living out *Orange is The New Black* in real life. Minus the lesbian part, because I've just never been one to swing that way, personally.

Here's what I realized along the way when it comes to karma, revenge, haters, criticism, and all of those negative vibe things in life… LET IT GO. Harboring that much negativity, hate, judgement, and maliciousness inside of us is just a breeding ground for bad things to happen.

I know how much you think ruining her life would make you feel better. I know that you want to get back at him so bad it makes your skin crawl. I know that you want to tell off the people out there telling you that you are wrong or that you aren't good enough. I know you'd love to flip the middle finger to all of the haters out there watching you. But that would be the easy way out. The quick fix. The vice-like response that simply will not last. Nothing good will come from reacting in any of these ways in the long run. Not one damn thing.

Sure, I imagined how amazing it would feel to take a baseball bat and swing it as hard as I could at every single one of those Silverado taillights. I imagined lifting that bat up with all of my might and smashing it down on his rearview mirrors. And of course I pictured myself doing it with a fan blowing my hair back. I pictured my legs looking amazing in red bottom stilettos with my perfectly smooth, tan skin in a sequined miniskirt. Oh, wait, I'm not Carrie Underwood belting out a top country music hit? No, honey, you'd be the girl in the apartment complex parking lot in leggings and a hoodie getting handcuffed and thrown in the back of a squad car in Southeast Michigan instead.

All jokes aside, though…trust me. I know how good it feels to envision these scenarios in your head after all the pain and hurt they've caused you. You want to give all that pain back to them times ten. You want them to feel how badly you feel. I know in the moment you feel like giving it all back to them will make it all go away and feel better. But the truth is…it won't. And you might even end up sharing a toilet and a cell mate when all is said and done. No, thank you. I like my privacy a little bit too much for that.

Truly ask yourself, what does revenge accomplish? What does going after someone to get them back truly accomplish? Five minutes of pride? Not worth it. Feeling some sort of short-lived satisfaction? Knowing that you gave them a taste of their own medicine? Don't lower yourself to their level, sweetheart.

When I was in high school, I was part of the party girl crowd. I was popular. I don't say it to sound conceited or full of myself…but I was. I was on the Homecoming Court with the sash over my shoulder. I was plastered all over the yearbook photos. I dated popular guys. I was at every party every weekend. I always dressed cute and looked perfect every single day for school when everyone else was in sweatpants. I was that girl. Always.

When I think back on high school, there are obviously a lot of things about that time that make me want to cringe. I think we all feel that way about our past choices from time to time. Whether it's the fashion statements we chose to make, the way we acted, the things we said, or how we embarrassed ourselves in front of the whole school…we all have things we wish didn't happen from those four years.

One particular time that always hurts like a thorn in my side is the one time I was a really mean girl. I was surprisingly friends with pretty much everyone in school. I was nice to the weirdos, the nerds, the band kids, the popular kids…I was just an overall friendly person as I always have been. I even came in second place in the Senior voting for "Should Have Been A Couple" with one of the gothic guys in school that had long hair and wore all black because I was always so nice to him. But there was one time in high school that I can look back on and realize that I was a f*cking MEAN girl. It was not my prettiest moment.

There was a girl a year younger than me that a lot of the girls didn't like. Honestly, the way she acted kind of brought it on herself. She chose to cause drama constantly and even messed around with peoples' boyfriends. She was just THAT girl. Long story short, she decided to give a blowy to one of our friends' boyfriends. We all found out. We all were pissed. We were hurting for our friend and we wanted to make her life a living hell for what she had done. Plain and simple. We went into girl gang mode and our eyes were set on hurting her the way she had just hurt our friend. The claws were out and we were ready to fight.

I'd like to point out here that we went after HER and not HIM... Immature. Catty. Plain old naive. Stupid as f*ck. Further allowing that guy to think it was okay to treat women that way. Which I'll bet he still does...but we were young. Clearly, we weren't mature enough to really see the situation for what it was.

So, we found an extremely unflattering picture of her on her MySpace (hoping you're all old enough to remember MySpace), and we made flyers to put around the school. I don't remember what was typed above the photo but I remember we added something not so nice about her. We put those flyers in all of the girl's bathrooms, in the gym locker rooms, in the hallways, in lockers, and basically anywhere else we could put them. We were gonna show her that you shouldn't mess with this clique...

When I think back on that day now, it literally turns my stomach. We were f*cking MEAN GIRLS. We were being cruel. We were lowering ourselves to a whole other level. We were maliciously trying to hurt someone else. We went out of our way to try to get back at her. It was straight up BULLYING, something I am one hundred percent against. Knowing that I did this still makes me cringe to this day. I hate thinking that I was ever a bully, but on that day that's exactly what I was. I was a f*cking bully over a loser sixteen-year-old's blow job.

But the bottom line is that we were BULLIES who went for REVENGE. We lowered ourselves to a whole new level of sh*tiness. We had zero class about it. We were horrible girls. We were the girls that are portrayed in movies that every hates. The girls that would make someone go home and cry and not want to come back to school again. I was a part of that, and I'm ashamed of it still to this very day.

So, what did we accomplish with our big poster making act at school? Nothing. She didn't change. We didn't go back in time and prevent the blow job from happening. He was still a loser. And we almost got suspended from school. So what did we accomplish? Did we feel better? Did we make the world right again by being bad people? Nothing. No...and no. All we did was lower ourselves to another level as young women, hurt someone, and bully someone.

Now that I'm older and more mature I can see that nothing good was ever going to come from that situation. Nothing about going out for revenge against someone is going to make whatever happened go away. It's not going to solve the big problems in your life and it's not going to make the bad feelings go away either. Revenge is a petty, mean, and negative thing. It is immature and ugly. It's a shallow and nasty thing. That's exactly why we need to leave it alone.

What I've learned is that it is far better in life to be the bigger person, take the high road, and kill 'em with kindness and class. Do not stoop to their level. Do not bring yourself down to the low vibe place they operate from. Hold your head up high. Put one foot in front of the other. Know that what is meant to work out will always have a way of working itself out. And also know that karma is real, and she's one hell of a b*tch.

Let's dive into karma next because I operate on the belief that it is so very real. I believe that you get what you give one thousand percent. I believe that bad people attract bad things things like a magnet, and that good people reap good things. I've seen it in my own life and in the lives of others over and over again. It's an idea that I've landed on many, many times when I've felt that stirring to get revenge after being hurt. Karma gon' get 'em.

Call it the law of attraction. Call it, "You are what you surround yourself with." Call it, "What goes around comes around..." I do believe that we attract exactly what we put out into this world in life. If we are kind, genuine, and compassionate, we will bring more good things into our lives. If we are malicious, negative, and hurtful, we are absolutely going to bring in more low-vibe, negative things.

So when I think about the people that have come at me from a low place, I just trust that the Universe, God, and any other Higher

Powers out there have got my back. They'll take care of it for me someday, somehow. I may not even know what will happen, but that energy doesn't just go away. It'll catch up to those bad people one day while I'm living a beautiful and happy life, saying "Cheers!" with my virgin pina colada retired on a beach somewhere.

Should we talk about the haters now? Let's dive right in because we all will experience them at some point in life, especially if you have the internet and an opinion of any sort. There will always be people that won't like you, what you're doing, and what you have to say. It's just a part of life. There is always going to be someone out there that just might not like you for any given reason. Don't take it too personally.

I actually loathe the word "haters" because it makes me think of some kind of conceited, self-entitled twenty-year-old giving a label to anyone that doesn't agree with them. Yelling, "Haters gonna hate!" while throwing up sideways peace signs with their hands outside of the club bragging about how many bottles they just bought…Also, you know if you're around my age at all, you have taken a photo with your hands in that sideways peace sign trying to look cool. Welcome to the '90s and the 2000s.

So, while I loathe the word and the person I envision saying it in my head, the whole idea of haters is actually pretty valid. Haters are always going to hate. They are always unfortunately going to exist. People are always going to have something to complain about, something to dislike, and they are going to want to voice their opinion on your Facebook timeline if you share anything about your political stance, religious stance, or your love of using profanity in all of your content…Yes, welcome to my life. That's just what happens when you decide to be yourself and include the word "f*ck" in just about everything that you write. Someone is always going to have their panties in a twist about it.

The important thing to realize is that haters, or negative people in general, are going to be hateful and negative people. Sometimes no matter how much we wish we could, we just can't change their mind or how they feel. So let them bask in all of their negative energy and let 'em be.

Just because there are haters and negative people out there it doesn't mean that we have to entertain them or let their opinions into our lives. We don't have to allow all of that hate into our lives. They are allowed to have their opinions and live their life the way they wish, but we can absolutely live peacefully alongside them and not have to be a part of it.

One big thing I've had to mature and realize growing up is that not everyone is trying to hate on you if they offer you an opinion or guidance that you don't agree with. People are allowed to have different ideas than yours. There is a very big difference between hate and advice, or even constructive criticism in some cases. People will sometimes offer you advice that is different from what you're thinking and there's going to be a lot of times you just won't agree with it. But it doesn't necessarily mean that your way is right and theirs is wrong.

There have been so many times people have offered me "advice" about how I could do things differently that they think would be better for me. They've offered me pure, raw criticism about all of my work. People have told me I'm a sh*tty writer. People have criticized my love of the F word. People straight up don't like some of my podcast episodes because I talk about a lot of super touchy subjects. But here's the thing: people can give you all of the criticism they want and it doesn't mean that anything you're doing is wrong. It's just your way of doing it. You don't have to change a thing about who you are and what you do because someone else thinks you should do it differently.

I've definitely had to have a thick skin when it comes to being in the online space and writing as a part of my career. I've had to accept this idea that people are going to hate on me. People are going to have an opinion of me. People are going to criticize me. Having a thick skin and staying on my level and not lowering to theirs has been key to keeping me sane in this journey. Having the same attitude of thick skin and staying on your own level is the same advice I have for you as well.

Be the bigger person, stay in your own lane, and keep on truckin', sister. I can promise you that living in this way will make you happier, healthier, and allow you to enjoy your life a whole lot more. Don't worry about petty things like revenge, haters, and criticism. Don't even waste your time on them for one minute of your day. You just keep doing you and living that beautiful life of yours. And always remember: KARMA gon' get 'em, so you don't have to. *Peace sign*

THING #8 | NOBODY CARES ABOUT YOUR CELLULITE & YOUR MAN JUST WANTS YOU NAKED

These bodies of ours are temples. I know you may be cringing at the cliche-ness of that phrase because you've heard it a thousand times. But there really is a bit of truth behind that statement. Honestly, think about all of the things that our bodies do. For God's sake, THEY MAKE TINY HUMAN BEING VERSIONS OF US, INSIDE OF US. That alone right there takes the cake for me. The fact that because of the birds and the bees, our bodies have the ability to smash together a sperm and an egg, cook it up into a human being the size of a pumpkin seed, and grow it inside of us for NINE months before shooting it out of our lady parts and into the world. Ladies and gentleman, I give you childbirth!

But all joking aside, think about your body…Think about all of the things it allows us to do and be throughout our lifetime. It's absolutely incredible. Mind-boggling actually.

Every little bit and piece and part of our bodies has a purpose and a reason for being exactly what it is, doing exactly what it does. From the heart that pumps blood through our body to the ever-annoying hair that grows around our nipples occasionally, every little thing has a purpose and a job. Try to remember that next time you're contorted into seven different standing positions in the shower to shave all of the unsightly hair that grows out of our bodies. Also, please be especially careful around those delicate little nips, baby girl. Trust me, an accidental aloe-rimmed, triple blade razor to the nip is not the most enjoyable experience. They bleed a lot more than you would expect them to, and I may or may not have walked around for half of a day with a band aid inside of my bra for that exact reason.

We, as women, are so critical on our physical bodies sometimes that we completely forget all of the incredible, amazing things that the body can actually do. We tend to focus more on those last ten pounds we never lost, if our belly rolls over our jeans when we sit down, and making sure we choke back two tablespoons of apple cider vinegar every morning while gagging because we heard it can help us lose weight. What we should be focusing on is how these incredible things covered in skin work and all of the insane things that they allow us to do!

We all tend to hone in on what we think is "wrong" with us physically. We stand in front of fitting room mirrors with horrible fluorescent lighting examining that pair of skinny jeans from every angle to see if it makes our butt look like J. Lo's. We poke. We prod. We grab. We shake. We b*tch. We moan. We complain. We whine. Then we proceed to scroll through our Instagram feed where we get overloaded by perfect Instagram models with *ss implants who look like they have eaten nothing but romaine lettuce tossed in lemon juice for the past three years straight. No wonder we spend our days thinking we need to constantly change something about our bodies to feel good about ourselves.

I had a diary when I was a pre-teen and teenager that I used to write in and keep in a lockbox hidden away under my bed. It was during that horrible awkward stage where you're thirteen years old, you've got little buds starting to grow on your chest, and your eyebrows just look f*cking terrible because you tried to tweeze them by yourself for the first time. Add the fact that your body decides to start bleeding out for week at a time without killing you, and you've got a perfect cocktail for some seriously shaken young female self-confidence. But back to the diary....

I had this diary that I remember FILLING the pages with of things about myself that I wanted to change. I would write about how I thought I was fat. I would write about how the cute, popular boy that was my "boyfriend" at school and I broke up. I would then go on to tear myself apart physically and name all of the ways I wanted to change things about myself on the outside. Maybe if I cut my hair this way...Maybe if I started wearing different makeup... Maybe if I only ate dry cereal until dinner and got really skinny...I always finished these ideas with something along the lines of "Then maybe I'd be happy."

When I think back about that young girl sitting on her purple and lime green flower-covered bed with her N'SYNC CD single playing on repeat, listing out all of the ways she thought she needed to change her physical appearance to be happy, it literally makes me want to cry. I should have been out riding my bike to the pool with my friends and having our moms drop us off at the mall to spend our allowance on a basket full of clearance accessories at Claire's. I shouldn't have been feeling this way about myself. I shouldn't have been listing everything I wanted to change about myself in a diary while crying and feeling like I wasn't pretty enough to everyone else.

I can even vividly remember trying to make myself vomit in the bathroom a few times with the water running so that nobody would be able to hear. I shoved my finger down my throat multiple times but just couldn't do it. I hated throwing up more than anything, but I was sitting on my bathroom floor crying with the water running and my little fingers down my throat because I thought that if I could just be a LITTLE bit skinnier, I would be happy...

Fast forward through my teens and twenties, and that attitude was still somewhere inside of my young adult head. I can thankfully say that I never tried to make myself sick again and I never actually starved myself, but I still had that underlying idea that I told myself about how being skinny would make me happy. I would go through all of the fad diets, meal replacement shakes, Lean Cuisine frozen Mac n' Cheese lunches, and working out religiously for over a decade. Always chasing after that elusive "perfect" image I thought would finally make me happy.

When I got older and started getting into serious relationships, sex just brought about a whole new kind of body image self-consciousness. Lights turned off, sheets covering my naked body, and only the positions that make my body look its best, please. Alcohol helped to drown away some of my physical insecurities when it came to getting naked with someone of the opposite sex, and I often leaned heavily on it to feel sexy and desirable. If you've read any of my previous books, then you know that this only led to bad choices, a lack of judgement, and virtually no inhibitions once I was blackout drunk. All that together was a cocktail for disaster.

I'll spare you guys all of the in-between parts and jump right into the main ideas I learned along the way when it came to my body and my appearance. There are two main things I learned that really settled in at the end of my twenties that I can give you guys:

1. Nobody gives a sh*t about your cellulite.
2. Your man just wants to see you naked.

These two little ideas are worth their weight in gold when it comes to backing off with the criticism and accepting yourself exactly as you are. Because first of all, they are both SO true it's not even funny. And also because over time, you'll start to see just how true they both are in your own life.

Nobody gives a sh*t about your cellulite. Nobody is going to sit around at the beach and point to the dimples on your thighs and say "OH MY GOD. CELLULITE!" The young, tan, super-hot lifeguard who is probably twenty-three years old and loves the fact that he gets paid to see boobs all day in tiny bikinis is not going to use his binoculars to hone in on the stretch marks on your hips from birthing a baby human being. Seriously, people just don't give as much of a sh*t about it as you probably do. Most of the time they won't even notice it.

Ninety-nine percent of women in the world will have cellulite. Even the super fit girls I follow on Instagram with amazing bodies own the fact that they have cellulite too. I love it SO much when I see them post unedited photos of their cellulite on their thighs or their tiger stripe stretch marks on their *ss. Not only is it vulnerable and inspiring, but it tells the women out there that they are human and they are not exempt from having normal bodies just like the rest of us. Just because they look great does not mean that they are superhuman and excused from dealing with the same body sh*t that ALL of us deal with.

I have absolutely LOVED seeing how the media has started to change and challenge this idea. I am living for the magazine covers that will now feature women of all shapes, colors, and sizes like Ashley Graham and Lauren Chamberlain. It makes me so happy to see all women being embraced as strong and beautiful, no matter what size or shape they may be. It's about damn time it happened.

It has been much needed and very much overdue that we started showing women not only as young adults, but at all ages, that we are beautiful no matter what our bodies look like or how many dimples they have on them. It's about time we focused on our strength, intelligence, and drive in life more than the jean size we wiggle our butts into on a daily basis.

I've learned to stop obsessing about the last five pounds or the fact that my jean size has gone up in recent years. I've told myself "You know what!? You've got someone that loves every inch of you to death. You've got a man that loves your body so much as is that he wants to put a human being inside of it one day." Think about that!

I've learned after years of making sure I did regular hardcore workouts and had a great body for showing off to guys at the bar that that was never going to be what got me the type of man I wanted to spend my life with. The people who truly want to be a part of your life will want to be a part of your life no matter what your body looks like.

I've learned to love this body and cherish the fact that it allows me to live and move. I've learned to appreciate the fact that this body will allow me to give life, and that cellulite doesn't have a damn thing to do with that. I've learned as I've aged to gracefully accept my body the way it is. I stay healthy, of course, stay active, and eat healthy most of the time. But I also never deprive myself of anything just for the perfect jean size. It's just not worth it in the grand scheme of things.

The world will not stop spinning on its axis and you will not be able to accomplish anything less in life because of a few extra pounds, a dimply *ss, and touching thighs. End of story. Celebrities have em. Your best friends have 'em. You have 'em. I have 'em. We all have 'em. And the bottom line is, nobody cares about your cellulite as much as you do. So learn how to embrace it and wear it with unshakable confidence. Own that body, girl.

Your man just wants to see you naked. Seriously, picture this scenario in your head right now. You met Brian on whatever dating app you randomly swiped right on his fine *ss profile pic on. You flirted over text messages for about a week. He took you out on an amazing first date and the sparks were FLYING. I'm talking electric sparklers were going off between you two over the table. IT. IS. ON.

You guys start to physically get SUPER attracted to each other, because its 2018 and people tend to get naked with each other rather quickly nowadays. You start making out at your place, one thing leads to another, and you're tearing the clothes off of each other. He stops, turns on the light, and screams, "I JUST CAN'T DO IT!" while pointing at your left boob, which you have hated all your life because it is slightly smaller than that right one. He puts his pants back on, says he'll call you tomorrow, and runs out of your apartment. You never hear from him again and you drown your sorrows in a *Grey's Anatomy* marathon with six bags of potato chips and French onion dip.

Are you f*cking kidding me? That would literally NEVER happen. I don't care if hell freezes over, there is absolutely zero chances of that scenario actually playing out in real life. Whether you are dating, married, or whatever, a man just wants to see you naked and is not spending one half second of his time looking at your body and criticizing the tiniest flaws that you imagine to be way bigger of a deal than they really are. That's not how it works.

Men are not as critical on our bodies as we make them out to be in our perfectly ombred little heads. They really could care less about things like imperfect nipples, mismatched boob size, and anything less than a perfect *ss. Men love women of all shapes and sizes. Men are probably just so hype that they get to be with a woman that they are not going to spend a second of that time doing a visual scan of your body with a checklist in hand to make sure everything measures up and is proportionate and in line.

Now let me get into preach mode real quick. If you guys haven't noticed yet my ability to be the no-bullshit, raw, honest truth preacher is definitely on the top of my list of life skills. I'm about to lay out some truths here that might even make you question the man you're with, so be prepared.

If a man ever says sh*t about your physical appearance in a negative, demeaning, or emotionally abusive way...then you need to pack up your sh*t and go. If a man says things about your body that make you feel ugly and self-conscious...then he is not the man for you. If a man EVER tells you that you need to change things about yourself for him to love you...BOY, BYE. Don't let the door hit your dumb *ss on the way out.

Men than demean, belittle, and put down women physically are insecure, Napoleon-syndrome battling, pathetic excuses for the XY male chromosome. You wanted to know the things I learned before turning thirty? Well, here's one of 'em! Men that behave in a way that carries the intent of putting a woman down and telling her she isn't good enough because of her physical appearance have no place in the life of today's woman. Kick 'em out. Get rid of 'em. Goodbye.

I was watching one of my terrible reality shows last night (and obviously forcing Andrew to watch it with me), and a scenario similar to the one I just described played out in the episode. An ex had been brought onto the show to stir things up in the young woman's new love connection. The piece of sh*t ex came onto the show and proceeded to belittle this sweet, beautiful girl in front of everyone, calling her "disgusting" and saying she "looked like a twelve-year-old little boy." Y'all…MY BLOOD BOILED.

Of course the new guy stood up for her and the insecure fool tried to throw a drink on him and fight him, because, hey, its reality TV. But what I noticed was how that sweet young woman crumbled. She absolutely fell apart. You could tell that he had done this to her for years by how his words triggered her to break down immediately. She cried hysterically to her new man and was literally shaking as she said that he was always so mean to her, just like this. You could just see how he had damaged that young woman for years and broken her confidence completely. It was heartbreaking.

Now I'm not saying a man can't make comments about how he loves when you wear your hair up. I'm not saying he can't tell you that you look great in anything black. That's a general opinion. But what I'm saying is NEVER in any way is it okay to belittle a woman and make her feel like she is ugly. It is never okay to tell a woman she should lose weight or change something about her physical appearance. And there is NEVER a time where using hurtful words to describe her appearance is acceptable.

If you've got a situation like this happening in your life, it's time to look at it and ask yourself if that's really love. If you've lived through a relationship like this in your life you are probably SO grateful that it is behind you. Ladies, never forget your worth and your value and NEVER allow abuse of any type to allow you to feel less than as a woman. Someone out there will love you…every "flaw," every dimple, every pound, every bad hair day, etc.

When I first got the photos back from the shoot I did for the cover of this book, the first thing I noticed was that I've gained a few pounds lately. I also zoomed in on the fact that my baby wrinkles on my forehead are definitely here to stay. I don't know if it's my age or what, but for the first time ever…I felt truly beautiful regardless of those things. I didn't stress about the fact that I looked curvier than normal. I didn't obsess over the wrinkles. I looked at myself in those photos…and I was happy. I was smiling. I was chasing my dreams. I was fulfilling a bucket list thing for myself to be on the cover of a book. The pounds and the wrinkles didn't matter. I was beaming with true inner and outer beauty and real happiness. I thought to myself, "Girl, you look amazing."

What I've learned about my body is to live with acceptance. I've learned how to love my body for everything is it for me. I've learned to cherish this body exactly as it is for the things it allows me to do. Wrinkles, cellulite, extra curves, and all. I've realized that nobody is examining my body like I do in the mirror. And I've also learned that some dimples and fat don't make me any less of an incredible woman.

I've also found a man that feels that way about me, too. I've learned that true love doesn't care if you gain a few extra pounds from eating out a lot during a busy week. True love will load up on the couch with you and dip pizza in ranch at the end of a long day without a care in the world. And they will never, EVER say a damn word about you ordering the dessert bread with the icing on top because you were feeling like treating yourself. They will love you exactly as you are…even while you've got icing dripping down your face in sweatpants. Which is exactly the way you should feel about yourself, too.

THING #9 | I LIKE MAKEUP, LASHES, & NEW CLOTHES BUT I'M STILL BEAUTIFUL WITHOUT THEM

So to carry on from the previous body-loving, self-confidence focused chapter, here's another thing I have learned regarding my appearance as I'm coming in hot on thirty. Doing a full face of makeup makes me feel beautiful. Getting my lashes done makes me feel beautiful. Wearing a new outfit straight off the rack that fits just right makes me feel beautiful. Styling my hair makes me feel beautiful. Every single one of these superficial things that I spend my time and money on makes me feel beautiful. But, do you know what else makes me feel beautiful? Taking off my makeup at the end of the day. Putting my hair up in a scrunchie knot while I'm cooking dinner. Wearing sweatpants. Getting into my pajamas at 5pm.

I think a lot of us as women can think about a time period in our lives where we wouldn't DARE go out of the house without makeup on. For some of you, that time might be right now. It might still be a thing. You might not be just yet ready to bare it all in public yet. I felt that way most of my teenage years and for most of my twenties as well. I would have never entertained the idea for one minute of going to the mall without foundation, lashes, contour, and lip liner over-lining my lips a la Kylie Jenner. I mean, what if the man of my dreams was there shopping and saw me in my bare skin and natural face!? *GASP*

Maybe it's because I stopped giving as much of a f*ck about the things that I realized really weren't important as I got older, or maybe I've just gotten extremely comfortable with the skin I'm in. At some point before thirty, I've realized that this is the face, hair, and body I was born with. Why was I SO intent on covering it all up to look different? Why was I so focused on changing what it naturally looked like constantly? To look just like everyone else? To look like someone that I'm not? Why do we all want to look like the exact same version of perfection that we have made up in our heads and in society today?

A lot of it definitely has to do with our confidence. It has a lot to do with how we feel about ourselves and how accepting we are of ourselves just as we are. "Flaws" and all. "Imperfections" and all. I use both of those words in quotations marks because they aren't actually real. They are just the ideas and criticisms that we have created about ourselves in our heads. They are the things we've pointed out and decided are "wrong" about ourselves. But in reality, we all look different and have different features, so it's not possible for things to really be flaws or imperfect. There's no way to judge something about how we look as "right" or "wrong."

I used to focus on contouring my nose like a psycho because I thought it was too big and I hated the bump I had from breaking it as a teenager. I used to think I needed the newest "it" bag to look classy and like I had made it. I used to wear lashes every single day because I thought my own lashes never looked as good. I felt the most confident when I was done up to the nines. Perfect hair, extensions, perfectly applied full face of makeup, and the most stylish outfit to strut. It would make me stand a little taller, hold my head a little higher, and walk with a little bit more confidence in my step. I felt beautiful.

Now, the tables have really turned for me. I actually get a little bit empowered to go out without makeup on. It seems funny to say that, but there is something that just feels good about letting my skin breathe, feeling natural, and not wanting to cover it all up. Something about it makes me feel stronger and more confident as a woman. How could something so basic and simple feel so life changing? Probably because for so many years it felt so wrong.

For years it felt like if I wanted to feel good I needed to cover myself up and primp and prime myself to look perfect. Why did I feel like showing what I really looked like was such a bad thing? Why do a lot of us as women feel this way on a daily basis? It's really quite sad to think about it from the outside looking in. Why do we feel the need to cover up so much of who we are and what we look like before the world sees us like it's a bad thing?

Now I have to interject here and say, don't think I'm throwing all of my makeup away and never washing my hair again. Don't think that I'm cancelling that lash fill appointment I have set up in a week to get my lash extensions done. And don't for one second think that my online shopping habit is going to go away, because, girl, that would be like the apocalypse happening. Literally there's a better chance of Starbucks going out of business than there is of me giving up all of these things in my life.

I mean, I do have a small business that I run in the beauty industry, which I absolutely love. I truly enjoy being a part of that industry so much. The beauty industry is fun, creative, and all about expressing ourselves through art with our hair and makeup. I paint women's faces for their wedding days every weekend of my life, and my appearance can sometimes be my best business card when it comes to making women feel glamorous and beautiful on their big day. So, yes, I make sure to look the part for my beauty business. That way my clients aren't terrified as their stylist shows up to make good money styling them with no makeup on and the scrunch I slept with in my hair from last night lopsided on my head.

So, don't for one second think that I'm saying that I'm giving it all up. That's not gonna happen. Also, don't think for one second that I'm telling you to give it all up. NEVER. A girl's gotta have her pretty little makeup and extras on her vanity. But what I am suggesting is finding a balance and a sense of your own natural beauty with or without all of the extra things. Find out how to enhance and embrace rather than cover and disguise. Ya feel me?

Are you comfortable with your natural beauty? The way your skin looks after a rested night of good sleep? The way your hair dries naturally? The size of your lips? The shape of your face? The freckles that show once you've been in the sun for a little while?

Literally for the first time in my life, I can say YES to all of these things. It certainly did not happen overnight. It took a lot of growth and acceptance on my part. I think a little bit of laziness and not giving a f*ck as much really helped it become easier as well. I've just stopped worrying about the judgement of others in my life. Life is too short to be worried about something so silly in the bigger picture of things. I've stopped worrying about what people might have to say about my bare face at the corner drugstore. This is the skin I was born with people. I'm just wearin' it.

I had spent so many years of my life looking for the things to make me look perfect. The things to make me look "beautiful." The things to make my skin look flawless, my lashes unnaturally longer, and my body look more toned. The things I could use to cover and disguise what I was born with to make it into what I thought was a more beautiful version of it. The things I could inject into my lips to make them look bigger. The things someone could use to cut open my nose to make it look smaller. The things a doctor could put into my boobs to make them look bigger and sexier.

I literally had every intention of getting a nose job the day I turned eighteen when I was younger. I also said I would totally get a boob job because my boobs were so small. At such a young age I was already planned on making major surgical changes to who I was… and for what? To feel prettier.

THIS was my mindset and my thought process when I was just a little girl...A LITTLE FREAKING GIRL. A little girl that should have been daydreaming about being a NASA astronaut or a race car driver just like her Barbie dolls were. A little girl that should have been excited to chase after her big dreams in life. A little girl that should have been out there experiencing her life confidently rather than comparing herself to airbrushed faces in magazines.

Instead I was a little girl that spent hours trying to make her hair look perfect for school. I was a little girl that needed new outfits to feel like I looked cute enough for school. I was a little girl obsessed with the idea of making my nose smaller, my waist tinier, and my boobs bigger. I wanted hair extensions, fake nails, and a fake tan at all times. I was a little girl convinced at a very young age that looking perfect on the outside equals happiness on the inside.

How sad and how warped is it that this is what LITTLE GIRLS are worrying about? Not about lemonade stands and hopscotch designs with chalk on the driveway, but how they can look more "perfect" to everyone else in the world. Buying things and changing things about themselves to be different just to feel good about themselves. To feel like enough and to feel good enough. How did we get it THIS wrong?

I hope and I pray that women can start to see their true beauty more often and at a younger age. I know we all have that awkward stage and rite of passage when we are younger where we just have to try out all the things. I had that whole stage as a preteen that involved buying every frosted lipstick sold for 99 cents at my local drugstore. I also went through a time span when the Bath & Body Works roll on blue raspberry scented body glitter doubled as my eyeshadow on a daily basis. Makeup was fun and innocent then, not a disguise and a necessity to go out in public. And that's exactly what it should be... fun. Never a disguise.

I've gotten back to this place where I see makeup, hair, clothes, and everything else extra as fun again. I enjoy putting it all on for a date night or when meeting friends for dinner. Some days I wear all the extras. Other days I don't add much to my natural appearance at all. If you guys are followers of mine on social media than you've seen me post Instagram videos absolutely makeup-free pretty much daily. You've seen YouTube videos of me when my hair is in a knot and I'm in my sweatpants. You've seen just how comfortable I've gotten over time with my natural beauty.

I posted a photo last night on my Instagram where I had substantially less makeup on than I would have ever worn in the past, especially for a social media post. It wasn't one of my many super styled, perfected selfies….it was just me.

I've done this a few times in recent months and each time it really reminds me how far I've come with accepting my natural beauty. I know how far I've come because I feel just as beautiful in these more natural photos as I ever did in my full glam hair and makeup selfies that I used to post constantly.

The weird part is, I noticed that the people that followed me on Instagram seemed to come out of the woodwork to like and comment on these newer, more natural photos. These photos literally got more attention and kind words and likes than any of my other photos I've ever posted. People left me the most heart-warming compliments on those photos, and the word "beautiful" was a part of many of them.

Who would have thought that after all of the perfectly styled photos I have posted over the years that these would be the ones that drew this type of attention? The ones where I didn't look "perfect" in society and the beauty industry's eyes. The ones where it was me… natural, authentic, raw, and beautiful all on my own.

But what I notice the most about these photos is the feeling I get from them. There is something so raw, so freeing, and so empowering about posting a natural photo of yourself. I don't see the new foundation, the glowing highlight, and the perfectly styled hair in these photos…I see ME. I see a woman who has finally embraced her natural beauty. A woman who doesn't need a makeup routine of thirty-two products daily. A woman who doesn't care if her hair just air dried and has a little frizz. A women standing so true in herself and in who she is without all the extra things. A woman who feels f*cking beautiful exactly as she was made to be.

THING #10 | EVERYTHING WILL PASS

It was a Tuesday. I was six months sober. I had just gotten home from work and took things out of the refrigerator to start making dinner. My then boyfriend always came over after I got home from work and I would cook us dinner before he went to work. He had planned a special vacation for my birthday, a cruise to the Bahamas, and we were leaving in several days. We had just went shopping for a floppy sun hat over the weekend because I absolutely had to have one for my amazing birthday cruise. My suitcase was laying open on my bedroom floor, half packed. The floppy sun hat laid next to it as I didn't want it to get crushed in my luggage. I couldn't wait to go on this trip. I couldn't wait to lounge in the sun together, eat amazing food, see amazing places, and have some time for just us. I could just see myself basking in the sun with my extra floppy hat in my bikini. I was so excited to go on this amazing vacation with him. I put a pan on the stove and turned the dial for it to start heating up.

While I was at work, he hadn't been responding to my texts like he normally would. Something felt off. I could feel it in my gut. I even messaged someone mutual to make sure everything was okay, and their response was something along the lines of, "They always do this…it has nothing to do with you…" from what I can remember. That response had my stomach in knots, but I tried to ignore it. There had been a TON of drama around that time with he and the mother of his child, but there was no way that it was going to break us….right?

I should have listened to what my gut was trying to tell me. My gut was trying to tell me that something was wrong, but I pushed that thought out of my mind. There was no way this was ending. I was just reading into it. I was being crazy. I was giving myself something to worry about when nothing was wrong. I mean, we had literally just gone shopping for our vacation the day prior and we were both so excited for it. I reassured myself to not worry. He was coming over for dinner, we would talk, and everything would be fine…

My phone dinged and I glanced over at it. I could see it was a long text message. I clicked it open and there it was: a two-page long text message…explaining that he was leaving me. It was cold and emotionless. It was straight to the point. I felt like I was reading something from a stranger who may have accidentally texted the wrong number. It even ended with him telling me something about how if I could give him the name of someone else that could go on the cruise with me, he had already called ahead to make sure that he could change it. He said that would be his, "gift" to me. Oh, how thoughtful and premeditated.

My stomach dropped to the floor. I reacted without even thinking about what I was doing. I turned off the stove, ran out of my apartment to my car, and started driving. I was speeding down the expressway in the direction of where he lived. I was having a full blown panic attack. There was a rock in my throat that felt like I could barely swallow. My hands were shaking uncontrollably on the steering wheel. I could barely breathe. I called my best friend at the time and my mom, and was choking the words out through tears "OH MY GOD…WHY IS HE DOING THIS…WHY IS THIS HAPPENING…" while I sobbed harder than I ever have in my life.

He wouldn't answer my phone calls. He wouldn't answer my texts. I ended up parked at his place, but he had already changed the code to get in (which I always had known so I could get into the house). He had locked all of the outer glass doors so that I couldn't use my keys (that he had made for and given to me) to get inside. The house was black. I didn't know if he was locked inside pretending to be gone or not.

I texted him: "Do it face to face. I deserve that at least." I stood in the driveway for a short while, pacing back and forth. I probably looked like a f*cking crazy person. I felt like I was losing my mind. I then got into my car and tried to figure out where his best friend lived from his house so I could drive by and see if he was there. After about an hour of aimlessly driving his city, sending texts with no response, and crying until my eyes were painfully red and swollen, I gave up. I went home.

I finally did get a text back around midnight. My mom was at my apartment because she came over to stay the night with me after hearing how upset I was and she didn't want me to be alone. We were both lying in my bed when the text came through. It was him. Cold and emotionless, just like the first text had been. Telling me how "unacceptable" it was that I showed up at his house unannounced. I don't remember the exact wording now, but he sent something saying that he hoped in the future he wouldn't have to be concerned about "unwanted invasions of his home."

I was shocked. Our text messages had changed from "I love you," hours prior to heartless accusations that I was an unwanted intruder of his home...like I was a stranger. Like I was a thief or a criminal. Like I was someone that you would call the police on for trying to come into your home. Like I hadn't spent nights watching movies with his child on the couch eating popcorn before they went to bed. Like I hadn't opened gifts during Christmas by the decorated tree. Like we hadn't spent Saturday nights trying out Pinterest recipes and then laughed hysterically when they turned out to be epic fails with his child. He finished that last text message reminding me that if I could give him the name of someone else to take on the cruise he already made sure he could call ahead and change it. I responded with a simple, "F*CK YOU."

It was over. I didn't know it at the time, but I would literally never hear his voice or receive another text from him ever again. I would receive an "anonymous" comment a year later on one of my blog posts with the alias name of one of his favorite movie characters. While I have no actual proof that is was indeed him that left the comment, I'm also not a f*cking idiot.

He even had the balls to say, "Until the last rose dies..." at the end of the comment. He had given me a bouquet of roses when we first started dating with one fake rose in it saying he'd love me until the last rose died. You can imagine the pure rage I felt when I read that "anonymous" comment on my blog and all the details led me to highly speculate that it was him. I chose to delete it and not even entertain any sort of response. He didn't deserve it.

He would again send me a message on social media two years later to tell me that "Happiness looks good on you..." I remember opening it in shock as I walked into the Fox Theatre in Downtown Detroit with Andrew and my family to see a Christmas show. I showed it to Andrew and I literally could not believe he actually felt like it was okay to reach out and contact me. This time I did respond. I replied with "Do not message me ever again" and blocked him immediately after deleting the message.

That night he left me, I ended up lying awake most of the night. My mom woke up periodically to see if I was asleep yet. I tossed and turned the entire night. I remember staring up at the ceiling for what felt like hours. Totally numb. Totally blank. Nothing. I cried occasionally, but I think I had gotten to the point that there were no more tears that could possibly be produced from my red, swollen eyes. I was broken to nothing.

THIS was the absolute worst breakup of my life. It would influence the way I felt about every single man I would meet afterwards. To say that it f*cked me up would be an absolute understatement.

I feared that anyone I truly loved would leave me, and I had an insane amount of trust issues when it came to men's exes. Although I've been told that there was no cheating and no going behind my back, you can't imagine what it felt like just a few short weeks later to have someone send me a photo of he and his ex on vacation in the same state we'd planned to fly into for that cruise. Again, while I have no proof, I speculated and put two and two together in my head and realized that he probably couldn't refund the plane tickets, so he took her with the tickets instead…with the tickets that were for MY birthday trip that would have happened just days after he had left me.

I was struggling emotionally and mentally. I loved him. I saw my future with him. We had talked about things like marriage. I loved his child like they were my own. I put up with more drama from his ex than anyone ever should have to in a relationship. He promised me everything. He assured me that he would have children with me because I had my heart set on having children. I spent holidays with his family. I bought everything to make and decorate Christmas cookies with his child. We took family photos on holidays wearing silly holiday hats. I furnished his child's bedroom with my old furniture when he bought his house and had left all of the furniture with their mom. He had been there for me during some really rough times. He held me while I cried in bed during really bad episodes of depression. He supported me in my early sobriety. I had loved him so much and so deeply, and he had always assured me that he felt the exact same way for me.

Heartbroken. Destroyed. Confused. Numb. Enraged. Belittled. Embarrassed. Humiliated. Angry. Spiteful. Livid…but mostly, just broken.

There are things that happen in your life that will cause you to sit there with your face in your hands asking yourself if you'll ever feel better. There are times in life that your heart will feel like someone just ripped it out of your body, threw it on the floor, and ran a lawn mower over it. There are times in your life that you will feel more hopeless and helpless than you ever thought possible. Rock. Bottom. Broken.

I've been there. I've laid awake at night staring at the ceiling with no tears left to cry. I've felt the guilt of not knowing what could possibly make things better. I've asked God "How much longer will this hurt?" many, many times.

It's not only breakups, it's losing people you love, screwing something up that can't be fixed, hurting the ones that care about you, and even almost losing your life because of your addiction to alcohol and drugs. There are going to be many times in your life that you are faced with things that feel absolutely horrible. You're going to wonder when will this pass? And one thing I've realized so far in this life is that no matter how much it hurts everything WILL eventually pass.

The days will get easier and the pain will start to ease up. You'll still have the moments where you will cry. You'll still have the moments where it HURTS. You'll still have the moments where things will cause you to cancel plans, stay home, and curl up in bed with your dog and a box of tissues. First of all, never underestimate the power of an early night in bed with your furbaby. As women, I think this is like our own personal therapy session in pajamas.

It will get better. It always gets better. And eventually it will pass. You've just got to have faith and believe that it will. Time will continue to go on. And while it's both fortunate and unfortunate, time is one hell of a healer. That's a good thing because it gives us hope that it WILL get easier as time passes. That's unfortunate because time is exactly that—time. You've got to actually live through it and let it go on. You can't speed it up, fast forward it, and you don't have a time machine. It would be so much easier if we had one, but you've got to allow it to happen as it happens.

Day by day. Moment by moment. The pain will lessen and the tears will dry up. You might even get to a point that you can forgive. I like to think that it's possible to forgive, but never to forget. I say to never forget because the experiences we go through in life build us.

They build us, and teach us, and change us into who we will be in the future. We learn and we grow and we take the experiences and the things we have gone through to use them, share them, and help others with them. If we never experienced difficult things in life, we wouldn't gain the strength that we do with time. Experiences build and shape us, both the good ones and the bad ones.

The hard times and the difficult times in our lives are what I like to refer to as our dark times or our own personal "winter" in life, because they will always pass. Just as light always comes after the darkness. Just like spring and summer always come after winter. Time will always continue to pass. Emotions will always continue to pass. Everything will pass. Just like the sun rises and sets or how the seasons continue to progress throughout the year…Everything will always continue to move, progress, and pass.

I'd like to add in here that I have come to my own type of personal peace with what happened in that situation with my ex. What he did to me broke me, but it also gave me strength. It gave me grace. It gave me the opportunity to show that one big bump in the road couldn't derail me in life. It tested me in my earliest sobriety, a time where reaching for the bottle to numb out the pain would have been an easy and quick fix. It challenged me to forgive someone that I felt did not deserve it one bit. It forced me to say that I was happy for them that their child had their parents back together, "one big, happy family" again. It tested me in many, many ways. It tested my strength and showed me what I was capable of handling in life, and for that I am grateful.

For what it's worth… I don't harbor any ill will towards these people or their family. They are great parents and they love their child very deeply. She is a mother that has raised an amazing and beautiful child that I was fortunate enough to experience and have a relationship with…and I want her to know that. She deserves a wonderful and beautiful life where she is loved and appreciated for who she is as a woman and as a mother. I hope that he is able to give that to her for the rest of their lives.

Sometimes things happen in our lives that feel like they are the end of the world. The truth is…they're not. Every difficult time in our life is put there for a reason. Whether it's to teach us something, to reroute us in a new direction, or to show us what we are really capable of handling in life, they are always for a bigger reason and a bigger purpose that we might not even be able to see.

Trust in that. That there is always a bigger reason for the things that happen in our lives. It's not just bad luck, a curse, or God trying to ruin your life…There's always more to it than that.

No matter how low you feel. No matter how broken your heart is. No matter how much it feels like you will never get through it…one day you will.

I've learned this time and time again in my own life so far. Things like waking up in an Emergency Room, getting your heart broken to pieces, losing people that you love so dearly…They will always pass. They might still invoke some sadness or negative emotions at times. They might still give me a knot in my stomach when I relive them in my mind, but they all have passed.

When I'm in a moment where I feel like something is so bad, so trying, so dark in my life…I always stop and remind myself of this. I stop, take a few deep breaths, and remind myself that this will pass. This will be something I write about or talk about one day without tears filling my eyes and without sadness washing over me. One day I will see and understand the bigger picture of it. There is always a light at the end of the darkness. There is always summer after the end of winter. There is always good after the bad. Trust in that. Trust in the idea that no matter how bad sh*t gets, it will always pass.

THING #11 | HOLD ON TO THE ONES THAT STUCK AROUND THIS LONG

When I was just a little babe, I lived in your typical middle-class neighborhood down the street from the park. The brick houses were close together and lined the streets evenly. Neighbors on neighbors on neighbors. I spent most of my summers on my bike riding to the corner and back until I was allowed to cross the street. I lived across the street from a girl just a few months younger than me, and her name was also Sarah. I heard the story many times about how our moms had met and shared that their daughters had the same name, lived on the same block, and were born just several months apart. The Universe seriously couldn't have lined this one up more perfectly if she tried.

Sarah and I would talk on the phone every day from across the street. I knew her landline phone number by heart, and I actually could still rattle it off right now without a problem if I had to. We would stand on opposite sides of the street every single day and yell across to each other until one of our moms looked out the front door and told us we were safe to cross the street. We had lemonade stands all summer and saved all of the money we made to go get back to school manicures. We swam together at the community pool down the block almost daily. We had themed sleepovers regularly with our American Girl dolls. Front lawn gymnastics with the newest hot cassette tape playing was a definite favorite activity of ours. We even orchestrated a haunted house every Halloween in my backyard with our older siblings and invited the entire neighborhood. Me and my girl Sarah were thick as thieves.

I remember the day my family bought a house and we moved away. I remember crying so hard that I couldn't breathe and I remember seeing Sarah run down the street after our car crying. My mom still says to this day that seeing that broke her heart to pieces.

We were crushed that we no longer lived across the street from each other. I'm not even lying when I tell you that at twelve or thirteen years old I would ride my bike all the way back to my old neighborhood every single day of the summer and call my mom when I got there to let her know I made it okay. Nothing could keep me and my Sarah apart. We went to N'SYNC concerts with homemade signs, we went on vacations together, we had our first crushes on boys together, we made our own Babysitters Club flyers for the neighborhood together…we even experienced death in our families for the first time together. We did everything together.

As we got older, our lives changed and drifted apart a little bit. We definitely ran with different crowds once we got into high school. I became the wilder of the two Sarahs. We dressed differently, hung out with very different people, and became teenagers that were not exactly the almost identical, innocent Sarahs that we used to be. We were growing up and figuring out who we were, and we were not following the same path in our young adult lives.

Even though I turned into the party girl while Sarah was the one involved with band and Church, something always remained in our friendship regardless. We never completely lost that connection we always had no matter how different our lives were. There was even an occasion where Sarah took her dad's car while they were at Church to come pick me up from a guy I had been dating's apartment while I sat on the curb in last night's outfit crying. I didn't know who to call and I was stranded, so of course I called my Sarah. And of course she came to my rescue. Because as different as we were, we were still the Sarahs from our childhood deep down.

That was us. Through it all. We were so different, but we still never completely split. No matter how much we started to drift apart. No matter how much things changed, we always stuck around in each other's lives. Through thick and thin.

Here's the thing…We never weren't friends. Sarah and I never completely fell apart from our friendship. No matter how much things changed we were always still there for each other. We were together for every death, every breakup, every loss, every celebration…

I stood on the altar when she got married and she was still the first text or phone call I made whenever big things were happening in my life. Even now, turning thirty years old, we still call each other every time something big is happening in our lives. We now started a tradition where we have breakfast together on every Christmas Eve morning with her husband and Andrew.

She did move out of state a few years ago, and you know my *ss is patiently waiting for the day she moves back. Because we have a whole adult life to live and navigate together now! We have future babies to raise and play dates to have! I'm not going to lie, I've always secretly hoped that we would have teenagers that fall in love and get married. The saga of our lives together could just continue forever then.

No matter how much our lives changed or shifted, we were always still there for each other. And I know that we always will be, no matter what happens. Because Sarah is that person for me—the one who stuck around. The one that never got tired of my ways or judged me for the bad choices I made in life. The one who never wrote me off like she could have many, many times in the past. She was even the one who got in contact with my mom the night I ended up in the Emergency Room and almost died. Nobody else knew how to get in touch with my mom, but they got a hold of Sarah because they knew she'd be able to.

I found a letter while packing up my townhouse for Andrew and I to move into our first home we bought together. It was dated on my birthday from back in 2007, the year we graduated from high school. I don't remember what was in the letter I had written to Sarah first, but it was something along the lines of apologizing for how I hadn't been a good friend to her in high school. She explained that she felt like she had lost me for a while in the letter, but that she was so excited to see that she was getting her friend back. The letter was a reminder of how Sarah has always been towards me, and of the person she has always been in life. Kind. Loving. Compassionate. Someone that always stuck around.

There are certain friendships in your life that you know will be a part of it for the long haul. The women that never turn their back on you. The women that show up when everything is going wrong. The women who stick around regardless of how much your lives have changed. The women who don't judge you when you go through your rock bottom stage. The women that go through all of life's stages with you. The women that love you unconditionally throughout your life, no matter what. These women live out the meaning of what a sisterhood should look like.

THESE are the ones you hold onto. THESE are the ones you cherish. THESE are the blessings and angels in our lives disguised as friends that take a place in your heart and in your life forever. Hold onto them.

CHERISH these people. These are the special ones. These are the ones that God, the Universe, and all the Higher Powers out there sent to you to be a part of your story. Think about it...of all of the millions and trillions of people in the world, THESE people found you. You found these people. Stars aligned and things came together just so that these people became a part of your life. You could have never met them. One little decision or thing in your life could have been changed and they would have never been a part of it. But they are. They were meant to be a part of it.

I've had many friendships in life that didn't stand the test of time. They didn't make it through the changes, twists, and turns. Some of them ended on a not so positive note. Some of them were really disappointing to watch fall apart and fade away. Not every person you meet in life will remain a part of it. Some friends are meant to share a part of a season or two, and then go on their way. Know that they were meant to be a part of it, but maybe they just weren't supposed to be there in the long haul.

After I got sober, I saw my friendships change in more ways than I ever imagined they would. So many things about my life changed during this time, including who would still be a part of it. I lost a lot of "friends" during this time. Some of the friends I lost were a lot more disappointing than others. There were some people I thought would be the ones that stuck around, but sadly, I was wrong. I had to just accept it. I had to realize that some people weren't meant to be a part of my new life.

While I did lose some of the friends I thought I would always have, sobriety also showed me who were the good ones. Obviously my Sarah was always one of those people. But I really started to see who the other really good, meaningful friendships in my life were.

I realized who genuinely wanted to spend time with me on a random weekend night staying in. I saw who was always on my team and always clapping for me when good things happened in my life. I started to notice that I had real friends that didn't need to go do something social to spend time together. I realized which friendships had real, deep-rooted connections that would last the test of time and all of the big life changes. I held onto those people...my own personal tribe.

I remember when I turned sixteen. I had a birthday dinner at a local Mexican restaurant I loved. I invited and had like thirty girls from my high school come to it. It was my version of a lavish sweet sixteen party but in a way that seemed more appropriate for someone living in a southeast suburb of Detroit. I was just trying to live my best life at sixteen, sue me. Anyways, I look at who was there now and I don't even talk to like ninety percent of those people. Some of them I wasn't even really that good of friends with. I honestly don't even know why I invited them, except for that I wanted to be popular and "cool."

I was on Homecoming Court in high school senior year, and I was so excited! I picked out the most beautiful, extra dress with handmade flowers appliqués flowing down the side to the floor. IT WAS AMAZING Y'ALL. It was like my own personal red carpet moment in Dearborn, Michigan. You know I was all about it.

But anyways, there I was so excited to be on Homecoming Court, every teenage girl's dream in high school. I had my hair done, my makeup done…the works. I scanned the crowd for my friends, and they were all sitting together. One of my "party girl" friends and I weren't friends anymore around this time. She had gotten the entire group of our friends to make signs for another girl on Court and not me. I remember standing in front of the entire school trying to keep the tears from coming out.

I walked off of the track at the football game after they crowned the queen and I saw my Sarah. I told her, "I'm so f*cking done with them" as one tear escaped down my perfectly made up face. These weren't real friends, and in that moment I realized that most of the girls I spent all of high school with didn't really care about me at all.

Situations like this have continued throughout my adult life. Thinking about planning a possible future destination wedding right now, I couldn't even give you a guest list of over ten women that I consider good friends and would actually want to be there. I'm not being mean and saying there aren't more than ten people that I consider to be my friends, I'm simply saying that destination wedding guest lists require you to get really cut throat with who is REALLY important to you. It really showed me how few people are in that inner circle of really good friends now at thirty years old. Eye-opening.

I never realized how much my friend circle would change as I got older until it started to really change on me. My circle got smaller. WAY smaller. I had much fewer close friends than I ever had in the past. Sometimes while watching *Sex & the City* or any other female-centered shows on TV, I would ask myself why I didn't have more good friends like the people on these shows. Why don't I have ten best friends that go on girls' trips to Aspen together like they do on the *Real Housewives!*? Is that a thing now?

Here comes the truth bomb. We already talked about how important the ones are that stuck around this long. They are the ride or die, lifers of friends. But, I learned to also be okay with the idea that the number of women that fall into that category in my life can be very small, and that that is NOT a bad thing. Your closest and best friends can be small in number, but so much larger in value.

I'd rather have a small, loving, in it for the long haul group of girlfriends than have a whole slew of women that don't love me as much. I'd rather have meaningful friendships with fewer women than to make it a popularity and numbers contest. Quality over quantity.

I'll say it again for the ones in the back...QUALITY over QUANTITY. You can have lots of decent friends just to have more people on your team, or you can have fewer more deep-rooted relationships that will really stand the test of time. That's what a true sisterhood looks like to me. I'm not saying I don't have a lot of friends in life that are awesome, but I am saying that my small, ride or die, girlfriends who stuck around this long are the ones I cherish the most.

Things happen exactly as they are meant to in life. You meet some people for a reason. These people are in your life for a reason. They are the ones that will stick around. Through the lowest lows, the highest highs, and the messiest of messes...these are the ones that will stick around for you. These are the people that have become worth their weight in GOLD to me. They have stuck around for me through ups and downs, ins and outs, and everything in between.

Find these people in your life…and hold on to them.

THING #12 | IF THEY WANT TO GO, LET EM' GO

There have been several relationships in my life that I clung to like I was Rose clinging to that door in the f*cking Atlantic Ocean in the movie *Titanic*. Literally there have been certain people in my life that I could not fathom not having them in my life at that given moment. I held onto them like my life depended on it. I stayed in relationships way too long. I put up with one too many liars and cheaters. I tried making plans with friends that showed they couldn't care less about seeing me way too many times. I guess you could say I was really not a quitter in that department of my life for many, many years.

I could have had a big shiny trophy and a gold medal around my neck when it came to trying to keep people around that weren't showing me they wanted (or deserved) to be there. Put me up on that podium and play the national anthem while you throw that medal around my neck, please.

Maybe it was my #codepencyissues, or the fact that I absolutely hated being alone. That's a WHOLE other chapter. No, really, it's literally the next chapter in this book. So we'll get to that topic shortly.

I liked stability in my life. I liked having the guy stick around. I liked having the friends that were around for the long haul. I mean who wouldn't want the people in their life to stick around? I think it's the kind of thing we all like and enjoy in our lives. Consistency. Reliability. Predictability.

But what about when these people don't deserve to be there? What if they shouldn't be sticking around? What if it's their time to go? What if they've literally shown you that they don't want to be there anymore? What if they are literally telling you that they don't want to be with you anymore? *GASP*

One big fat reality that I've learned in my lifetime so far is that if people want to go and leave your life...LET 'EM GO. I'm at a place now where I can confidently say, "Let me hold the door open for you..." when they show me they don't want to be a part of my life anymore. Clearly, that wasn't always the case. It took a lot of growth, a lot of maturity, and a whole newfound sense of self-respect to be able to get here. And it wasn't always easy and/or pretty.

As I've mentioned already, we like things that are constant. We like things that are predictable. We like knowing what's going to happen next. We like knowing that the sun will come up every morning, and that it will set again every night. We like knowing that our Starbucks latte will taste the same every time we order it. We like knowing that we have friends we can always call on. We like knowing that there is that guy that will always have a shoulder to cry on and an ear to listen. They are always on time and right on cue, and we like that.

Nobody likes to have the rug pulled out from under them, especially by the people that are a big part of their life. This could include your friends, your family, and your romantic relationships. These people are supposed to be safe. They are supposed to be easy and always on time. They are the lifelines of your life as far as relationships are concerned. The ones that shouldn't be pulling any fast ones and blindsiding you by leaving. But sometimes in life they just might do exactly that.

Sometimes people choose to go. It can be painful and hurtful when this happens. It can take you by total surprise and absolutely break your heart. We may try to hold onto them and keep them in our lives, because we aren't ready or okay with the idea that they don't want to be a part of ours anymore. But let's really dive deeper into this…

WHY? We might ask ourselves WHY they don't want to be a part of our life anymore but also, why would you want to keep someone in your life when they've shown (or even told) you that they don't want to be there? Why would you want to hold onto those people? Why would we want to hold onto someone who has slapped us in the face with the idea that they don't want to be a part of our life anymore?

When I think back on the times in my life that people blatantly showed or told me that they didn't want to be in my life and think about how I tried to chase or hold onto them now…it makes me feel like an absolute fool. It makes me feel pathetic. It makes me want to smack myself upside the head back then and be like "Girl, stop it."

This has happened to me the most in life when it comes to friendships and romantic relationships. I realized as I got older that people don't always want to remain a part of your life. I learned that no matter how badly you want them to stay or how badly you try to make them stay, it won't change things. When someone has their mind made up about wanting to go…they're gonna go. You might be able to delay or drag it out a bit, but when someone's mind is made up, it's pretty hard to truly change it.

I can remember men I dated breaking things off with me several times where I couldn't understand why and didn't want to let them go. I dated a LOT in my twenties and was an absolute hopeless romantic. I wanted true love. I wanted something real. For a long time, I was on an all-out quest to find a man that would be a part of my life forever. I used dating apps. I had friends set me up with friends. I constantly had one eye open watching for the man of my dreams to show up on his white horse wearing his shining suit of armor to whisk me away into our fairy tale love story.

When I thought someone could possibly be that guy for me, I tended to fall quick. I was all in on the idea that THIS could be him. You know what I'm talking about. You ignore all the red flags. You hang on their every sweet word and replay it over and over again. You have so much hope and excitement that MAYBE this could be the one. We get hooked on the idea that we want them to stay in our life forever.

When someone I felt like that about decided that they wanted to go, it sucked. I can look back and remember so many tears and pain. I can remember being so sad and so disappointed. WHY didn't they want to be a part of my life? I was a catch now! I had turned my life into an absolutely amazing one at the end of my twenties. I knew what I wanted and I was ready for it...So WHY did this person not want to be a part of it?

There can be many, many reason why a person chooses to leave. Whether it's a romantic partner, a friend, or even family, there can be many motivations for someone no longer wanting to be a part of your life. They can be good reasons or bad reasons. They can sometimes actually have pure intentions behind leaving. It might be hard for us to see it right away, but one day with some time and maturity you'll be able to see it more clearly in those situations.

Sometimes people don't romantically see a future with you, and that is why they leave. Sometimes they don't want to lead you on, and that is why they leave. They might know that things aren't going to go anywhere, so they get out early before emotions run too deep. As angry as we might be at them, you've got to have a little bit of respect that they end things before they got any messier or more painful. At least they ended things and didn't mess with your head for months and drag it along. That's what the real pieces of work choose to do instead.

Looking back, there are some men I WISH would have just left me. I wish they would have just let me live my life and not brought all of the pain, hurt, and chaos they brought into it. I wish they could have spared me the heartache, the tears, and the long lasting trust issues I got to keep as a consolation prize. But I also realize that each and every one of them was there for a reason and taught me many, many things moving forward in life.

I think we all get to a point one day with our past relationships where we can look back and understand them much better. We can see that it was a blessing in disguise that that person left us. We can see that our choice to leave a person was one of the best choices we could have ever made. In time we are able to better see why something needed to end, and actually be grateful for the fact that it did. You'll get there. I promise. If I could look back and actually be thankful that some of my biggest heartbreaks left me afterwards, then, honey, so can you.

There are also certain friendships that I WISH would have just walked away peacefully. Friendships where I wish we could have just acknowledged the fact that we no longer lived the same lifestyles and were okay with that idea. I wish that these people could have just walked away, let it be, and not done hurtful things on their way out. When you lose a friend and then they decide to openly bash you for the world to see, it's like pouring salt on the wound or turning the knife that has been stabbed into your back. But that's just the way some people live their lives.

When people show you or tell you that they don't want to be in your life anymore, listen to them. If you can part ways on peaceful terms and with a mutual understanding of why it needs to happen, that is the best way to go about doing it. I pray that that can be the way it goes for you when these things happen. There's been a few times I've been lucky enough for things to happen that way, but there have been many other times that it simply has not gone so smoothly.

I've learned that when someone shows you they don't want to be a part of your life anymore, you should listen to them. Don't try to fight it. Don't try to hold on and drag it out. Don't try to convince them otherwise. It just makes things messier. Let 'em go. Especially if they are telling you or showing you in a malicious or negative way.

There is no room for that kind of junk in our short time here on Earth. Be an adult. Handle your sh*t like one.

If people don't want to be a part of your life for immature or negative reasons, then they don't even deserve to be a part of it. Do them a favor and grant them their wish. Let 'em go. Wish them well. Don't let the door hit 'em on the way out. Don't waste your time on those negative people and those hurtful words and actions of theirs. Odds are if they are the type of person that could be so malicious and so mean so easily, they shouldn't be a part of your life anyways.

You will outgrow so many people and things throughout your life, that losing some people along the way will most definitely be inevitable. It is not necessarily a bad thing that some people just don't fit into your journey anymore. At one time they may have been the bread to your butter, the peanut butter to your jelly, or the one you ALWAYS pictured next to you in a bridesmaid dress. But that all can change as time goes on. That's a part of life that we all need to learn and understand. We change so much and take so many paths during our life and not everyone will always be a part of all of them.

So while it hurts and can be so sad for someone to leave, understand that maybe their time with you has just ran its course. Maybe they are not meant to be in this next chapter for a reason. Maybe they came into your life, lived out their time and their purpose, and now they are no longer meant to be in it anymore. Take that idea with grace. Understand that your lives are going down different paths and in different directions and maybe they just don't line up anymore. Even if it becomes a petty split with a lot of harbored negativity, find your peace within it. Let them go knowing that they just aren't meant to be in the next chapter of your life. And if there is any sort of hurt or pain caused by the other party, then be grateful that it is exiting your life. Welcome the next chapter of positive vibes with only the people that support them to the fullest extent.

Remember: You are an amazing, unique, one of a kind human being. You have characteristics and qualities that people out there love about you. You have people in the world that would LOVE to be with you. There are people who value their friendship with you more than you might ever know. Do NOT forget all of that just because of someone who doesn't realize exactly how amazing and bad*ss of a woman you are. Do not give someone else that power to make you feel less than or small. If they want to leave, let 'em go... knowing that it is what is best for you in the long run.

THING #13 | YOU MUST LEARN HOW TO BE OKAY ALONE

I used to f*cking HATE being alone. The thought of sitting completely by myself on a Friday night at home made my skin absolutely crawl. It literally made me want to cringe. The words that would pop into my head would be things like loser, party pooper, grandma, pathetic, boring, and so on and so on. Being alone was a foreign idea to me for a long time. I wasn't meant to be sitting at home by myself. I was meant to be living it up with all of my friends 24/7. I was so used to being the social butterfly climbing on top of bars and dancing on tables that the thought of solidarity on a Friday night seemed like the worst thing in the world that could possibly happen. It was like getting your eyebrows threaded, long and painful.

It can be a big fat red flag if you are unable to be alone. I discovered that through sobriety, lots of therapy, and lots of self-work. I honestly didn't fully accept and come to terms with this idea until after I got sober. When I finally gave up alcohol for good and decided to spend some time truly working on myself and not getting involved with any men for a while, it become painfully clear to me that this was something I struggled with. Weekends by myself were enough to send me into an episode of depression, and I knew that something about that was NOT okay.

For way too long I couldn't be alone. I would make plans with my girlfriends to avoid sitting at home. I would get in touch with a guy I might have not even really liked that much just to have company. (Can we say desperate?) I would go to my mom's house for dinner instead of staying at my own place by myself. I looked for every and any way to not be alone as often as humanly possible.

I can see this pattern when I look back at every area of my life. Whether it was family, relationships, friendships, or even my career... I hated being alone. I thought alone equaled bad. I thought alone equaled lonely. I thought alone equaled wrong. I'm not sure where I picked up this f*cked up idea, but it was a really hard one for me to shake.

One reason I do know that I hated being alone was that I didn't want to feel my pain or my emotions. I showed this over and over again when it came to my relationship status. If I had a breakup or a fight, I was immediately scrolling through my contact list to get in touch with someone else. There were times it would literally be the same day as a break-up, and I would already be contacting someone else just so that I didn't have to be alone that night. It wasn't even like I necessarily wanted to get into bed with them, I just needed them there so that I didn't have to face the hurt I was burying deep inside. It was also like my own little f*cked up way of saying, "Ha! You didn't break me..." by proving to myself that someone else wanted to be there still.

Trust me, I know I was being heartless and unhealthy with how I was living. It was self-sabotage at its finest back then. I was a f*cking pro at it. I was always doing the same things and then wondering why it didn't turn out differently. HELLO.

I had a pretty quick turnaround rate when it came to finding the next one. I could be single for 24 hours and I would already download all the apps again, already be in touch with the old ones again, and already be mentally checked out and onto finding someone new. The thought of being alone when it came to men made me cringe for a long time. Now, I understand why…

I was looking for other people to fill the voids in my life and to fix the things that were wrong within my life and within me. I was looking outward rather than inward. I thought that if someone was with me that I was fine. I thought that everything would be okay if I just had someone that wanted to be there. I thought that somehow down the line they would fill up the dark spots in my heart and that they had the power to fix all of the things I was going through.

The truth is, they were never going to be able to do any of those things. I was the only one who had the power to do those them. And I was going to have to do them ALONE. Accepting that was scary as sh*t. The idea was absolutely foreign to me and it took me a long *ss time to really understand it. I needed to learn how to stand on my own two feet and solve my own damn issues. Nobody else had the power to do it, it was all going to be on me.

Why do we feel like being single is such a bad thing? Why does being alone feel desperate, uncomfortable, and wrong to some of us? And why do we think that not being alone is going to solve all of our problems? So many of us depend on someone else to make us happy. We think that the puzzle pieces will fit and the stars will finally align when we find that person. We think that things will finally be okay. So many of us rest on this idea that when we find the one, it will make everything okay. Reality check, it won't.

We need to learn how to be alone. We need to learn how to walk without someone else. We need to learn how to love ourselves and be okay without someone else there with us. This can be much harder for some of us than others. I was definitely one of those people it was not easy for.

It took a lot of uncomfortable weeks and lots of struggling, but I threw myself into it. The first time I truly was alone, it was so weird to me. Me trying to sit at home all weekend and not contact anyone to keep me distracted and preoccupied felt like Bambi trying to walk on her wobbly *ss baby deer legs. It was so different and so awkward to me. I was so uncomfortable. But you know what they say, the things that make you uncomfortable usually teach you the most in life. And boy, was that idea spot on here.

The more and more time I spent alone, the easier it got. I realized that I was totally fine being alone. I also started to realize that it was silly of me to think that I couldn't be alone. I realized how much it could actually change me.

I spent a good season of my life pretty alone after I was about a year sober. I didn't have any actual romantic relationships during that time and I spent a lot less time out with friends. I felt a little anti-social at times, so I made sure to make dinner plans here and there just so I didn't feel like a total hobbit. But big things started to happen for me during that time period. If there's one thing that really stuck out to me during this time, it was the holy sh*t amount of self-growth that happened within my soul.

Being by yourself forces you to get comfortable with yourself. I mean REALLY comfortable with yourself. It forces you to be your own company. It forces you to do things on your own that you would normally do with someone else. It forces you to really accept yourself and who you are to the fullest extent. I feel like I learned more about myself during my season of being alone while sober than I did in my entire life. I also got super clear about what I wanted for myself and for my life. Clearer than I ever had been about any of it before. I became laser focused on what I wanted my life to be like. I created goals, I created boundaries, and I started to really see what I wanted for myself.

I made myself dinners for one. I binged entire seasons of shows alone. I traveled alone. I went out to eat alone. I read a lot of books. Personal development books, memoirs, and anything else that sparked my interest. I learned how to meditate. I tried out yoga. I went to be bed early and got the most amazing sleep every single night alone. I was truly selfish with myself every single day.

It felt weird and narcissistic at times, but only because I had never focused on myself so much. I realized that there was nothing wrong with it. I realized that it could actually be a good thing. And eventually I started to actually like it. It actually started to feel super empowering. I actually started to enjoy it. A LOT. Then I started to LOVE it.

This is just one area of my life that therapy helped to rewrite for me. I can't tell you how many times I had admitted to struggling in my therapist's office about something involving my being alone. She even hypnotized me once so that I could actually f*cking relax and not feel like I had to be doing something or with someone constantly. Did it work? Maybe. I just know that over time it got much better.

I've learned that the sh*t we need to work on and fix within ourselves is nobody's responsibility but our own. I've also learned that nobody else has the power to fix my problems, but me. Nobody else can step in and do the work for me. I had to do it all ALONE. I had to put on my big girl pants and get comfortable being by myself. I had to face the unfamiliarity and uneasiness of doing something that was super uncomfortable for me. I had to figure out all my own sh*t, JUST ME.

What it did was teach me that being alone is a powerful and transformative thing. It taught me how it could be a good thing. Something that shouldn't be avoided or made out to be negative. It could be empowering and beautiful. It could help me in more ways than I ever imagined.

In small ways and in bigger ways, learning how to be okay with being alone changed my entire life. It taught me that I needed to be comfortable with myself. It taught me that I could enjoy my life whether someone was around for every minute of it or not. It showed me that I could enjoy my own company for a change on a Friday night and actually enjoy it. It showed me that I could travel and explore new places with only myself and still see and experience amazing things.

Learning how to be alone taught me that I loved having people in my life, but that I had everything within me the whole time to be just fine by myself. It helped me make some life changing realizations you guys, LIFE CHANGING. And I realized all of them while I was (you guessed it) alone.

THING #14 | FAMILY IS FAMILY

We've all had those moments in life where you want to literally hide and pretend like you don't know who the crazy-*ss people who you call your family are. Maybe it was when your mom walked in on you and your first boyfriend making out. Maybe it was the time your sister accidentally flashed everyone her goodies in high school with an outfit malfunction. Maybe it was when your dad tried to be the cool dad and do something super funny in front of your friends that had you doing a major face palm. It happens. I know every single one of you can think of a time or a situation in your life that you stopped and asked yourself, "HOW can THESE PEOPLE be from the same blood as me?!" I've often wondered how I can be related to people that are so polar opposite of me in every single way. We've all been there. But like it or not, they are still your family.

What I've learned is that family is family. Biologically, you can't really pick 'em. You can't change 'em. And you really can't easily change who your family members are if we wanna get into all the technical, legal stuff here. I'm sure there's a sh*t ton of paperwork involved in that. Your family is your family, no matter what you do. There's a few gray areas for this one, which I'll get more into in just a second, but overall what's true is true. Family is family. Period.

I realized throughout the years that certain members of my family were the ones that always had my back regardless of how big of a mess I'd made...especially my mom. That woman is a damn angel and a saint for sticking around and putting up with thirty years of ME.

If you've read all about my past with alcohol in my other books, then you're familiar with how much shit my mom had to put up with throughout the years. I gave her an entire apology chapter in my first book because I realized what a lifeline she had been for me through the darkest of my dark times. She deserves a damn trophy for the woman that she is. Sometimes I wonder why she did it. But as I've gotten older I've realized that you don't just turn your back on your family when you love and care about them. You just can't.

My family and I are very, very different. I'm talking we couldn't be more different if we tried. It's one of those situations where you wonder how the one child possibly fits into this family. That child was always me. My family members are very responsible, they play it safe, and they've never understood half the decisions and choices I've made in my life. I have always been the complete opposite of them.

I was always the wild child, the risk-taker, and the envelope-pusher. I always took the big risks while they sat in the back and worried about how things would pan out for me. Sometimes I think people wonder how we could possibly all be from the same bloodline, but we absolutely somehow are.

I've learned that we can be total opposites and disagree on everything, but that doesn't make us any less family. Each and every one of us and our unique differences fits in our puzzle. We each make up a piece of the puzzle that is my family. It can be messy at times, but it somehow just works. That's what happens with family. We all accept each other's sh*t, love each other regardless, and somehow try to make it work out. And somehow it just does.

My immediate family members have always been some of the most constant things in my life. They put up with a whole lot of my sh*t and they never left. Anytime I had a big mess in my life, they were the first ones to help.

They've helped me financially when I was young. They helped me pay for college. My mom has talked me through every big life change I've ever made. My dad has been there to help me move into and do any handyman repairs in all of my places. My brother even let me live in his basement for a few years while I finished school after leaving my boyfriend that struggled with addiction when I was twenty-two years old with nowhere to go. They've just always been there for me, no questions asked.

My relationship with my family wasn't always easy, though. And you need to realize that yours won't always be either. They will get on your nerves, they will tell you their opinion on everything you do, and sometimes they just don't understand what you're doing at some points in your life and will feel the need to voice that. There were times my family made me want to literally pull my hair out and absolutely lose it on them. I butted heads with my family so much during my drinking days that I'm still shocked we made it out on the other end of things. There were a whole lot of fights. There was a lot of arguments and drama. There was just a whole lot of messy stuff going on back then.

I'll just never be able to say thank you enough and be grateful enough for my mom during my early sobriety. Even the day I walked out of the hospital after almost losing my own life, she greeted me with open arms. I was broken to pieces and falling apart and she knew it. She didn't yell or get angry at me. She just held me while I cried. She had me take a nap in her bed while she watched TV in the recliner right next to me. She sat with me for hours while I slept.

I'll always remember that day with my mom. My legs would make these spasm kicks similar to how you do when you have a dream that you're falling. It was probably just my body detoxing still from all of the drugs and alcohol that I had overdosed my body with. Anytime I moved she would lean over, touch my leg, and ask if I was okay with a worried look on her face.

I realized in that moment the undying love family has for family, and that my mother had for me. She was like a newborn's mother watching it sleep, terrified that something would happen or that her baby would stop breathing. I realized that I would always be her baby girl no matter how old I got. And I learned that she would always be my mom. Always there for me. Always loving me. Always taking care of me when I needed it most.

As I've gotten older my relationship with my family has really come full circle and its better than it's ever been. What I learned was that my family is my family no matter what happens. I learned to be grateful for them, because not everyone has a family like mine. Not everyone has two parents that are always there for them. Not everyone has family that all always help them no matter what. That made me realize just how grateful I should always be for mine.

Families are funny things. They can have some seriously f*cked up dynamics. They can leave you with serious issues in life. Family rubs off on you, there's no doubt about it. I've realized just how much my family influenced and had an effect on me once I got older. Some good ways and some bad ways, but there are lots of ways my family has influenced who I am and how I have lived my life.

We talk all the time about girls having "daddy issues" when they get older. I know people joke about it, but it's actually frighteningly accurate. Girls that grow up with absent or sh*tty father figures grow up to often have serious issues when it comes to the men in their lives. People that see their parents fight constantly when they are young grow up and that doesn't go away. Being treated poorly or abused by our family members when we are young stays in our subconscious mind for decades, and can affect us in all areas in our life forever.

Our families can definitely rub off on us more than we realize and leave us with some lasting issues. Thankfully, not all people go through this with their families, but a lot of people do. I've seen it in myself many, many times as I become more and more like my mother with every day that passes. I just pray I don't start using as much hairspray as she does on a daily basis. I'm not sure how she is able to breathe in her bathroom sometimes. I'm also really concerned for her safety any time she gets somewhat close to an open flame.

Something else I've learned about family is that it can also be made up of "family" that is not by blood. Your family can consist of the people that you care for as if they were your own blood.

Sometimes there are friends in our lives that take on the roles of and even double as our family. We feel just as much love and connection with them as we do our own siblings. They are just as much a part of our lives as our biological family is, and sometimes they can be an even bigger part of it.

What I've learned is that sometimes family isn't your family by dictionary definition, and that's totally legitimate. It's the people that are there for you no matter what. It's the people that care for you deeply. It's the people that are there for you every day. The ones you share every triumph and heartbreak with. The ones you can count on to always be there no matter what happens in life.

I've got girlfriends I would consider to be my sisters, absolutely. They have never judged me, never turned their back on me, and have always been a ride or die in my life. I've got friends that I've gone through deaths with, I've gone through breakups with, and that we've slept on couches together when someone was having one of the worst nights of her life. That's my family too, without a doubt.

I've learned that for some people, their friends have been a bigger part of their life than their own parents or siblings are. Some people in my life don't even have a relationship with their parents, and some have never even met one of their parents. For these people, family has a very different definition.

It's so wonderful to think that even if we are dealt a sh*tty hand of cards when it comes to who our family is, that there can always be other people willing to step up and fill those shoes. It's the silver lining of love and relationships. The idea that just because we weren't born as family doesn't mean we can't love and care for someone else just as deeply as if we were.

Andrew has a family that's the perfect example. The man that raised Andrew is not his biological father. Andrew's biological father is not a part of his life at all. At the time I'm writing this book, he has never even met him face to face. The father of Andrew's older brother stepped in from day one at the hospital and took over raising Andrew as his own. Can we get a round of applause for that one hell of a man? It takes a good man with a heart of gold to step up the way he did and fill that role.

To Andrew, the man that raised him is one hundred percent his dad. That is his family. It will be his father for the rest of his life. It doesn't matter what the details are, that man has always been Dad to him. In fact, Andrew refuses to call his biological father his dad. Even in conversations when I've referred to him as his dad he corrects me that that "isn't my dad." And it's true, the man that raised Andrew is absolutely his family no matter what. The fact that he is not biologically his father will never change that one bit.

So I've learned to cherish my family. I've learned that I am so grateful to have a family like mine. But I'm also very persistent about the idea that for me family goes far beyond just blood. It includes all of the people that deeply love and care for me, and vice versa. Family love you to death. Family always has your back and is always there for you no matter what. Everyone's idea and picture of who their family is can be different, but it doesn't change the fact that family is family. Period.

THING #15 | YOUR COMFORT ZONE IS A LIMITING LITTLE B*TCH

Everyone loves to be comfortable. You know exactly what I'm talking about. It's safe. Familiar. No surprises. Warm and cozy. Fuzzy blankets. Sweatpants. Homemade mac n' cheese… Okay so I'm definitely not going to be talking about the sweatpants and cheese covered noodles (yum)…But I am talking about the idea of our comfort zones. The place in our life where we color inside the lines, say please and thank you, and never go out of bounds. It's the place where things are always the same and are always constant. Things are always predictable and calm there. There's never any chances or risks taken there. In reality, there's nothing wrong with a comfort zone, per se. But I'm about to tell you all the things I've learned in life so far that are cons about staying inside of yours. (Hint: I've busted the f**ck out of mine!)

Most of my family members are what I like to call "play-it-safe-ers" as I've mentioned a bit in the previous chapter. They have always saved responsible amounts of money. They have always gone to college and made an honest earned paycheck. They've been active in the corporate world. They have all bought nice homes and new cars. They watch their credit scored religiously. They are cautious of things like debt and also about their health. And they have all also questioned just about EVERY decision and choice I've made on my own as a young adult woman.

You guys have undoubtedly already picked up on the fact that I march to the beat of my own drum in life. Being the only person pushing limits inside of a very safe and responsible family…Well, you already know how that played out over the years.

I remember my parents refusing to let me go to beauty school. They were helping me pay for a college education and made it very clear that they would NOT be funding my dream to work in a salon and do hair. I remember the day I told them I was going to quit teaching preschool just two months after receiving my Bachelor's Degree in Early Childhood (surprise!). I remember when I told them I was going to go-go dance in a nightclub in Detroit for EDM shows on the weekends. I remember when I told them I was going to move in with my boyfriend when I was twenty-one years old and he was ten years my senior with a breaking-down car, a drinking problem, and monthly child support to pay. I remember when I told them I was going to start a hair and makeup business as my main career. I remember when I told them I was going to write *Sober As F**** after getting sober. I remember them having their doubts and concerns about every single one of these things, as well as many other choices I made as a young woman.

You see, all of these things were not the "play it safe" route. My family in response was always worried about my choices. They questioned why I would want to quit teaching. They asked if I ever would want to get a "real job" with my degree again. They asked if I was going to be able to really make enough money to pay my bills working from home. They asked why I would ever put all of the details about my sobriety (including the not so pretty ones) into a book that anyone in the world could read. It was all risky, ballsy, and WAY outside of their comfort zones to do any of the things I was doing. It was all WAY outside of my own comfort zone as well. But that wasn't enough to stop me or hold me back.

I learned very quickly in life that doing things outside your comfort zone is a f*cking beautiful thing. Not only is it about taking chances and being brave, but it can take your life to amazing, incredible places you never thought possible.

Playing it safe can never take you to the places taking risks will. I now know that looking back on my life, every transformative and truly life changing thing that has happened was because of all the times I went outside of my comfort zone. It was because I took a chance and went for it. My comfort zone would have put a stop to all of it if I had let it. I realize now that our comfort zones can just be limiting little bitches.

Our comfort zones are limiting little b*tches because they don't allow us to stretch our wings in life and see what we are really capable of doing and achieving. They don't allow us to take chances and risk things. They don't allow us the chance to chase after living our dream lives. Our comfort zones never challenge or push past the things that hold us back such as fear, failure, or the risk of embarrassment.

Our comfort zone wants to keep us on that straight and narrow. Don't risk that. Don't allow yourself to be vulnerable. Don't try that without knowing what the outcome will be. No surprises. No chances to make an absolute fool out of ourselves. No chances to fail. But also, no chance to really make some big magic in the world.

When we can push past our comfort zone, this is the place where the magic can truly happen. This is the place where big shifts happen. This is where sparks fly and our outcomes are limitless. This is the place where we JUMP. We jump into the unknown. We jump into bigger opportunities and possibilities. We jump with our head in the clouds and our eyes aimed on the stars. We take chances. We risk things. We push ourselves to a place that is not our good old home sweet home.

It's unfamiliar. It can be scary. It can feel like we have no idea where we're going or what's going to happen. We're definitely not in

Kansas anymore, Toto. But do you know what happens? AMAZING, INCREDIBLE, BIG, LIFE-CHANGING THINGS.

There's a ton of quotes out there about how everything good happens once you get just outside of your comfort zone. I'm sure you've seen them plastered all over your Instagram and Facebook feeds regularly. If you're one of those people that rolls your eyes at those posts every time you see them, then you're probably already rolling them right now. But, roll with me here for a second instead. I promise to try to really make you see what I'm getting at.

If I never got outside of my comfort zone, I wouldn't be sitting here right now on a Friday morning in late August writing my fifth self-published piece. I wouldn't be editing the final touches of my next podcast episode. I wouldn't be mindset coaching women from all points of the world this morning through huge transition points in their lives. I wouldn't be watering the flowers I planted outside of our beautiful first home that Andrew & I bought together. I wouldn't have an amazing human being still in bed snoring with my Chihuahua. I wouldn't be planning a possible future destination wedding in Mexico. I wouldn't be running my own hair and makeup business. I wouldn't be receiving messages from people internationally telling me how my story of sobriety helped them have hope in changing and saving their own lives. I would have NONE of these things if I hadn't done something uncomfortable and tried something big.

Every time in my life that I pushed the envelope, incredible things happened. Every time I took a chance and did something my play-it-safe family thought was absolutely bonkers, big things happened for me. Every time I got outside of my comfort zone, I realized that I had no limits, no boundaries, and that I could literally chase after ANY crazy *ss dream I could conjure up in my pretty little head. I realized that the only limits being placed on me were the ones I placed on myself, or that I was allowing someone else to place on me. This got me on f*cking fire in my life. My head was spinning with ideas and dreams about all of the things I was capable of being and doing.

What scares the hell out of you? What is something that makes you absolutely terrified, but lures you in with the small chance at something BIG happening from it? Really think about it. What is something just outside of your comfort zone that you daydream and fantasize about doing, but never got the balls to actually try? What would you do if you knew you wouldn't fail at it? What is the little b*tch known as your comfort zone limiting you from going after in your life? What is she holding you back from?

This reminds me of the first time I did anything related to public speaking. I was absolutely shaking in my cute wedges as I drove to the venue. It was just a local women's meeting with probably twenty people max, but I was absolutely terrified. My nerves were out of control. I had hated even having to get up and give a presentation in college to the point that it gave me major anxiety. Public speaking was just not my cup of tea. Sure, I had no problem talking to my laptop, my webcam, or my phone to make social media posts and YouTube videos, but this was actual in-person speaking. Totally different.

I had been asked to come talk about my first book, *Sober As F****, to a women's group not long after I self-published it by a girl I had known for years. I said yes because how could I turn down the first time someone actually wanted me to come speak in any kind of organized setting about my first book!? It could have been two people sitting in a room and it would have still been crazy and unimaginable for me. It was humbling, exciting, and made me feel like a credible author for the first time in my life. But once the date of the meeting actually got closer, I got nervous as hell. What if I stuttered? What if I froze up and couldn't think of what to say? What if the women absolutely hated me or thought I was a total joke?

Public speaking was SO outside of my comfort zone. But guess what? I said yes. I pushed myself to do something new and uncomfortable, and that took some major lady balls on my part. And guess what happened? I f*cking did it. I stood up there, nerves and all, and I did it. It was one of the most fulfilling and transformative moments in my life and I had never felt more alive. All because I pushed past that limiting little b*tch of a comfort zone and did something amazing. I did something that scared the crap out of me at the time, and it changed my confidence forever.

I've learned that when we can get outside of our comfort zone, amazing and incredible things happen. The change your life type of things can happen. The magic happens. It's taught me to always push farther, dream bigger, and JUMP more. My comfort zone can try to intimidate me and hold me back, but that b*tch doesn't stand a chance here anymore. Cuz I'm here to JUMP.

For the first time ever, as you are already well aware of, I am on the cover of one of my books. Putting myself on the cover of this book was something I thought about for a while, but was never positive about due to my comfort zone. I had never done a photoshoot. The thought of posing in front of a camera and striking multiple vogue-like poses was not something I was comfortable with. I am no super model, sister. I am not used to lights, cameras, and striking a pose AT ALL. The only photo shoot I've ever done was my senior pictures and one other time a local photographer asked to take photos of me in downtown Detroit in my scantily clad go-go dancing outfits. Classy.

But guess what? Guess who pushed herself past her comfort zone, bought the cutest little LBD (little black dress) she could find, designed her own set, bought balloons, ordered a special pink cake, and paid for a real life photoshoot. Well, judging by the cover of the book you're reading, you already know the answer to that question: THIS GIRL.

I am SO happy that I took a chance and put myself on the cover of this book. When I got to preview the photographer's proofs for the first time I was literally beaming. I clicked through the photos like, "LOOK AT THIS B*TCH!" I saw a woman looking like a supermodel in those photos. Smiling. Glowing. Confident. Taking chances. Busting the f*ck out of that comfort zone. YAAAAAAAAS,

HONEY!

Now as I'm about to turn thirty, I welcome the opportunities to push outside of my comfort zone. I almost look forward to them. It's like I sit there and think, "What goal can I smash next?" I daydream about the next big thing I can do. I look my comfort zone dead in the face and say "Try me, Susan," when she attempts to surface and make her presence known.

I've decided that nobody gets to limit what I can do but me. And as you've probably already guessed, I will never be the one to hold myself back in any way shape or form in life ever again. And, girl, you've got the exact same power to do that too. To push past your comfort zone and do something truly amazing. Can I get an amen?

THING #16 | BE KIND, LISTEN, & BE THERE FOR OTHERS

In my twenties I worked a lot of jobs that involved working with the public. Being a hairstylist, being a receptionist, teaching preschool, and doing makeup professionally were all jobs that made me be around a lot of people a lot of the time. They also required me to listen to a whole lotta people and be nice to them. You know how people tell their hairstylist everything going on in their life? It's like they literally come in ready to update you with every single dramatic thing that's happened in their life since their last appointment. I'm over here wondering if Judy wrote it all down in a notebook somewhere so that she wouldn't leave one single detail out. That was literally my life.

Let's be honest, sometimes we just aren't in the mood to be "on" for others. You know what I mean. Smiling, listening to others, and showing constant kindness to everyone when sometimes you just aren't in the mood to do so. Sometimes you're just in a sh*tty mood. Sometimes you just feel drained. Sometimes you just ain't feelin' it today. Sorry Judy.

I found myself getting easily frustrated, not being as nice as I could have been, and just losing interest in putting others first a lot of the time. Sometimes I just didn't want to listen to people talk about their problems constantly at the salon. Sometimes I just wanted to mind my own business. Sometimes I wasn't up for listening to why a three-year-old was having a total meltdown over magnet tiles in a blue bucket in my preschool class. I was self-absorbed and I was too busy thinking about myself and what I would have rather been doing instead. Selfish? Yes. Young and immature? Totally.

Not so long ago I would still catch myself judging clients as I saw them from a distance, which is totally f*cked up to do. I'd see someone and immediately be rolling my eyes inside because I did not want to help this rude, loud, moody woman find the right foundation for her skin tone at my cosmetic counter job. I'd have already created the scenario in my head of how unpleasant having to interact with this person was going to be before they even got into my chair. Talk about being an *sshole.

I remember the first time I got reality checked with this truth. This woman was a mess from a distance. She was loud. She didn't have the most fashionable outfit on. She did not look like someone that I thought would spend $48 on a good foundation. I had already created this scenario in my head that she would say, "Hell no!" and go buy something at the local drugstore instead. Now, this was totally unfair and b*tchy of me to do, and I'm totally owning up to that. I've got no problem calling myself out on my own sh*t when I'm wrong.

She sat down and told me a few things about her skin. I got my brushes and a few products to test on her and we started small talking. She was in her 50s and had just been through chemotherapy. She went on to tell me about how she had also been through a horrible divorce a few years ago after her husband had cheated on her. She felt terrible about herself. She explained to me how she had lost all drive to take the time to get ready or even do her makeup anymore. She told me she felt horrible whenever she looked in the mirror at herself.

My heart absolutely broke for her. My eyes welled up with tears. I spent as much time with this woman as I possibly could talking to her and helping her find makeup that helped her feel pretty in her own skin again.

Why hadn't I just let this woman sit down and listened to her before I automatically judged her like a complete and total dirtbag? Why hadn't I led with kindness instead of criticism? I felt terrible about how I hadn't given her a chance at all. I also quickly realized how much my simply listening to her changed everything about her day. By simply showing this woman kindness, she was able to vent and I was able to hear her story and help her. It was like a pseudo therapy session for her to just have someone listen to her talk and let out all of her bottled up feelings and emotions. I felt so horrible... but I also realized how powerful just listening and being nice to someone can be. I realized how much kindness can really be worth.

You never know what you can gain just by opening up your ears and your heart. You never know just how much you can help or impact someone else's life by simply being kind. Simple examples of showing kindness can leave huge impacts on others. Something as simple as letting someone vent about what's going on in their life or their feelings can totally change someone's day. You can honestly be the bright point in someone's darkness just by opening up yourself and listening. How powerful is that?

What I've learned is that sometimes I need to not just think about myself in life. It's absolutely crucial to be there for others too. I've learned just how powerful it can be to listen to a client vent, take that phone call from the family member that needs to spill their emotions, or text that friend going through something rough just to check in and see if they are okay or need to talk about it. Just by being compassionate and being there to listen, we can absolutely do our part to make something better.

We can make someone's darkness brighter. We can be their something to lean on for support when they feel like they are falling apart. We harness that much power just by being kind, opening our ears, and opening our hearts up to others.

Listening and being there for others in itself is something I think we all could take a few more lessons on. We all tend to just want to stay in our own lane, put in our headphones, and walk down the street without making eye contact or engaging with anyone else way too often. We want to ignore everyone when we are busy and annoyed. We want to focus only on ourselves, our day, and what we are doing. This is not okay. Even if you are the biggest introvert, it still isn't okay. We need to open up. We need to stop worrying about only ourselves.

Any relationship needs people to listen. I know Andrew feels like it's probably nails on a chalkboard every time we get into an argument and I force him to listen to how I feel. It doesn't matter what is going on or what we are bickering about, I make him sit down, listen to how I feel and why I feel that way, and then I make him do the same thing back with me. I know sometimes it's the last thing he wants to do in that moment, but if we don't listen to other people, nothing ever gets heard, understood, or resolved properly. You guys, he probably hates me when I go all "Let's talk..." on him in the middle of a silent standoff. But I'm telling you it works wonders. Seriously, listening is one of the most crucial things in a relationship of any kind if you ask me.

Something that always comes to mind when I think about what I've learned when it comes to listening is the number of people that take their own lives...I always wonder if someone had been there to listen or for them to talk, would they still be here today? If someone had checked in on them, would things have gone differently? It breaks my heart to hear about every single one of them, famous or not. I always wonder if someone could have made a difference or stopped it from happening just by being there for them.

I've struggled with anxiety and depression for quite some time in my own life, and it got even worse when I first got sober. I know that sometimes that one phone call or that one text or email was the best part of my day. Knowing that someone out there cared enough to reach out made each day hurt a little bit less. I'm grateful for the friends and family that were there for me during my dark times, and I think they helped me get through some of those episodes just by reaching out to talk and to let me know they were there for me every step of the way.

Be someone's support system in a rough time. Be the shoulder to cry on, the phone call to listen to them vent, or just be someone they can count on. Be there for them when they need you. Show them kindness. I don't care if you're busy or have a million things going on, don't forget about the people in your life that need you.

I've had SO many women connect with me from around the world because of my first book, *Sober As F****. I've coached them, I've messaged with them, I've been someone to listen to them. I've always been there for them and I've always tried to respond to every single one of them that contacts me. Because I don't know if I might be the only one that's there for them in that moment. I don't know if my being there for them could change everything just by simply opening my heart to these women.

I've had the honor of running a sobriety group on Facebook for quite some time now, and I can tell you that being there for those women to listen to their struggles and help has been so humbling. Being able to be there for those women to give them a place they can feel safe and supported during rough times with addiction and alcoholism has been life changing. Being able to give them the reassurance that someone is there for them is the greatest gift I've ever been able to give. I often wish I had had a group like that when I was in my early sobriety.

I beg you to check in on the people you know that might be going through some sh*t. If you know someone that's going through a rough breakup, or a divorce, or recovering from some sort of trauma in their life, check on them. If you know someone is struggling to stay sober, check on them. If you know someone is having a hard time lately, check in on them. They need it more than you think.

Check on the people that seem to be doing just fine, too. Just because people aren't vocal about things doesn't always mean they aren't happening. Reach out with a simple "thinking of you" message or an invite to grab lunch and catch up. You have no idea how much having someone to talk to or someone to listen can change everything about how someone feels on any given day. So please, be there for people in the world. You might impact their life much more than you ever thought you could.

Be kind. I can't stress the importance of this enough. Simple acts of kindness can change someone's day. Simple acts of kindness can create a domino effect of other acts of kindness that will follow. Simple acts of kindness could truly change the world. Look for chances to be kind to every single person in every day of your life. Do something special for someone. Be the light in someone's day. HELP SOMEONE. I'm telling you guys, showing kindness to others can truly change the world. And it can start with little ol' you and I.

Open up your ears, your eyes, and your heart. Listening and being there for others can change so much about every single day of anyone's life. Showing kindness can do the exact same thing. It can make so many situations better and so many things brighter in life. You never know…just by being there, listening, and being kind you could even save someone's life. Maybe. Maybe not. But wouldn't it be better if we all starting living this way at the chance that it could save even just one? Remember that next time someone might need you. Be kind. Listen. Be there.

THING #17 | YOUR THERAPIST WAS RIGHT, COMMUNICATION IS GOLD

I know a lot of us women out there like to assume that our significant other, our children, our friends, and anyone else we encounter in regular life are psychics and mind readers. Our husband should KNOW that his clothes are supposed to go in the hamper, not on the floor in the bathroom shoved behind the door, right!? My mother should KNOW that I was too busy to answer her phone call five times in a row while I was on the treadmill, right!? I think sometimes our subconscious makes an assumption that everyone has a little bit of Miss Cleo in them and should know what we want, what we're thinking, and be able to read between ALL of the lines of our vague, condescending comments at all times. Unfortunately for us, that's not how people work.

Time and time again I laugh to myself about how I'm really getting my money's worth from my therapist's office when I catch myself communicating like a f*cking CHAMP. Sometimes I find myself really "using my words" (as they say in preschool) with

Andrew during a fight and I think to myself, "someone give me a couch to have this man lay on and tell me his problems."

So many relationships fail because someone can't communicate. I've seen it in my own life, and I've seen it in so many other people's lives as well. When people can't communicate to their significant other about what's bothering them, it just grows and builds and festers inside. It builds and builds until it explodes one day and you totally blow up about it, causing much more damage. I'm talking Britney in 2007 taking an umbrella to an SUV after shaving her head type of damage. So open up to the ones that you love. Tell them what you need. Tell them how you feel. Tell them what makes you happy. Tell them exactly what you want and what you don't want. SPEAK THE F*CK UP.

I've read it in a ton of books, heard it on multiple podcasts, and have heard many experts talk about how communication can make or break a relationship. I am all on board with all of these people. I've been the one to bite my tongue and not tell someone how they made me feel in the past. It seemed easier to just suck it up, ignore them, and be done with things than to actually sit down and talk. Rather than telling someone that they hurt me, I would just leave them. That worked out fine and dandy when I was a teenager and in my early twenties, but you can't be that naive and stubborn as an adult. I mean you can, but you're never going to get anywhere good in life that way.

It has been a huge game changer for me to learn just how important communication is. Not only in relationships, but in my career, in my friendships, with my family, and in just about any other situation you can think of. I've watched it change a lot of things in my life. It gave me the balls to ask for a lot of the things I wanted in life. It made me stand up for myself when something didn't sit right in my heart. It gave me a newfound sense of empowerment when I realized how much power I had in simply using my voice and speaking up.

It could have been something as simple as asking for a raise at work. It could have been telling someone that I wasn't comfortable going to a certain event after getting sober. It could have been leaving someone who failed to show me any respect at all. All of these times and all of these situations showed me that I had power and that I had a choice. A choice to communicate what I wanted and what I needed for myself. To stand up for myself and make my words heard loud and clear.

Communication is just KEY. First of all, nobody is ever gonna know what the f*ck is in your head unless you tell them. As I mentioned previously, people are not mind readers and they don't know what is going on inside of your brain. They don't know the thoughts going through your head and they don't know how you feel about something unless you speak up and actually tell them. Sometimes you've just got to break it down for them verbally. USE. YOUR. WORDS. GIRL.

Being in a successful and healthy relationship of any sort requires good communication constantly. If you aren't able to communicate, it's just never gonna work. Plain and simple. Whether you're just hooking up with someone and wondering where things are going, or if you're suspecting that your spouse is upset but aren't really sure exactly what you did to cause it... you've got to just communicate with them. Otherwise nothing ever gets solved and everyone is left wondering and trying to figure out on their own what the hell is going on.

How do I know this? Because for the first time in my life I'm in an actual long-term HEALTHY relationship. One of the biggest things I've done differently this time is communicating like a champ. You can ask Andrew how many times I've explained why I felt a certain way about something for almost two hours straight. A lot of times. I've realized the power of talking and communicating and I am using the sh*t out of it. Like I said, it probably gets on his nerves sometimes, but it's the best relationship that either us of has ever been in. That's gotta be saying that we're doing something right this time around.

If you're not amazing at communicating right away, give it time.

The more you do it, the easier it will be. I don't even think twice now. It's become a natural way of life for me. It's become the automatic response I take now when something doesn't feel right. It's become the way I express my emotions, my wants, and my needs on a daily basis.

This girl's emotions are being heard, and those wants and needs are being met finally. That's what happens when you stop biting your tongue and leaving things unsaid when they need to be said.

Leaving things unsaid is one of the worst things you can do in relationships. I've learned this over and over again. Have you ever not told someone how you felt about them, and then it was too late? Have you ever not told someone that something they did bothered you and just let it ruin whatever the two of you had? Has someone disrespected you and you kept quiet, only to have it continue to happen over and over again? I think we've all been stubborn and done this one time or another in our lives. Then you're stuck looking back wishing you would have just opened up your mouth and said something.

But as I'm telling you how important it is to communicate don't you dare think that that doesn't mean you have a responsibility to listen too. Listen to what your partner has to say. Listen when they tell you something hurt their feelings. Listen when they say they're unhappy about something. Listen to what matters to them and what is important to them. Listening and communicating are golden. They will help you SO much in your relationships. I promise it will be a game changer in every single thing you face.

As I mentioned earlier, communication is not only important in just our romantic relationships, but also in our friendships, families, careers, and just about anywhere else you can think of. Tell your friends how you feel. Tell them when something feels bad. Tell your family when they do something that gets on your last nerve. Tell your boss that you want more responsibility on the job. Voice your opinion and tell people how you feel about things. Just start talking more. Start communicating in all areas of your life. Start speaking up!

Therapy is a prime example of just how impactful and amazing communicating can truly be. That's literally all you do in therapy, talk and listen. It's all communication. The amount that therapy has helped me in the last few years is absolutely insane. I had no idea just how much I would benefit from it not only during my early sobriety, but still to this very day.

Once a week I go spill and word vomit everything in my head, communicate everything that's going on, and get it all out. It feels f*cking incredible. Having a professional to listen and talk with you and help you figure out your own sh*t...now that's just priceless. I would gladly pay much more than my insurance's $30 co-pay to do that once a week.

Even what I'm doing right now writing this book telling you about communication is technically communicating with you. I'm writing down all the things I've learned before turning thirty to share my story and share what I've learned with the world. I've done it in every single one of my books. I've used my voice for good. I've used my words to give hope. I've used what I have to say to help change the lives of others. And I've always made you guys laugh a few times along the way too, right? Go on and admit it. *Hair flip* I did all of those things just by using my voice and communicating.

So, what do you have to say? What can you do with your voice? Have you even started using your voice yet?

The power in what you have to say and in how you communicate it can be limitless. So don't only communicate with your boyfriend or your girlfriend, share your words with anyone that wants to listen to them. If you have a message to share and something to say, say it. Speak up. Use your voice. Share your story. Use your words. You just might give someone the inspiration to start saying what they have to say too.

It is such a beautiful thing to see when people stand up and start using their voices and saying what they need to say to the world. People will be there to listen. Give them something to hear.

So with this one what I've learned that I can pass along to you, it's to communicate and to use your words. Make your therapist f*cking proud! Use your words like an infant that just learned how to talk. TALK. TALK. TALK. Write the book. Record the podcast. Share your story on Facebook or Instagram. Inspire others with your words. Call a friend. Have that talk. Tell someone how you feel about them. Communicate what's on your heart and in your head. Say what you want and what you need. It all starts with communicating and using your voice. Try it. Speak up. Just watch how your life starts to change.

THING #18 | YOU'RE GONNA HAVE BAD DAYS, OFF DAYS, & FUNK DAYS

As I write this chapter, I'm in sweats on my couch at 4pm on a Thursday. I've got a hot cup of organic ginger lemon tea with extra ginger and raw honey by my side. I've got my fuzziest white blanket draped across my lap and my Chihuahua, Kaya, cuddled up to my side. I just made myself protein pancakes with mixed berry syrup (frozen berries and a tablespoon of syrup in the microwave for two minutes... you're welcome.) and am listening to some '90s music playlist while I write. I had planned to record multiple podcasts today. I had planned to crush my workout today. I had planned to go out to celebrate a friend's birthday tonight at a local bar (sober, of course). I even had plans to go shop for some cute fall home decor. As you can see, none of those plans happened...

I'm having a bad f*cking day. I tried to force myself to push through my run to make it go away. I tried to take Kaya for a walk to get some sunshine to boost my mood. I tried all my typical tricks to pull myself out of the funk I found myself in. Nothin'. I'm just in a complete and total funk today. I couldn't tell you why, and sometimes this just happens. No way of predicting when or why. It just happens.

I think a lot of us feel like as women we need to always be "on." We feel like we have to do everything and we have to do it perfectly. Some of us have so much on our plates everyday as moms, entrepreneurs, friends, etc. that we think we can't afford to have an off day. It might throw us off. We might not get everything done. We might not be the *Leave It To Beaver* mother having it all together while pulling a piping hot meatloaf out of the oven with our seasonally coordinated oven mitts.

Guess what? Sometimes we just aren't going to be able to do it all. We're gonna have a day where things don't go perfectly and we can't do it all. And that's absolutely okay.

I've figured out in life that sometimes we're just gonna have bad days. We're gonna have off days. We're gonna get stuck in these funks out of nowhere. They're lousy. They can be super inconvenient with all of the things we have or want to get done. We wish they didn't have to happen. And if you also suffer from any type of anxiety or depression…Well, sister, I'm right here with ya trying to weather the storm, too.

Sometimes these types of days just happen. We can try to fight them off armed with every podcast, every mindset shifting trick, and every self-care act in the book, but sometimes they just don't make it completely go away. Those feeling still fight their way through. It's gonna happen and there ain't nothin' we can do about it. At some point we've got to just stop fighting it and say, "Okay, let's just get through this."

When I was early on in my sobriety I noticed that I had a LOT of these days. That's honestly the first time I realized just how much of a presence anxiety and depression actually played in my life. I knew things bothered me sometimes, but that was nothing like the things I felt after getting sober. There were days I would just get in bed and cry. Nothing prompted it. Nothing bad happened. I would just get so overwhelmed with anxiety and emotion that I would shut off completely. I would feel depression to the fullest extent and it became absolutely exhausting. There were many nights curled up on the couch or in bed watching Netflix alone during that time. There were many worried phone calls from my mother during that time, too.

While suffering from any type of mental health situation isn't fun or enjoyable, I will say that having those rough days taught me a lot about myself. It really allowed me to better understand my emotions and how to process through them in a healthier way. I realized that fighting them or trying to deny that they were happening was just a recipe for disaster in the long run because eventually sh*t would hit the fan and I'd explode with an emotional meltdown.

I learned during this time that I had to just allow myself to really feel. I had numbed myself out with alcohol for so long that in a weird way, it almost made me feel alive again. As much as feeling the negative vibes and bad feelings sucked, I was oddly grateful that at least I was feeling things again.

It's kind of f*cked up to think about it, but I was almost welcoming the feelings with open arms in a way. Maybe in a way it showed me that I was growing as a person and changing. Even if it was shitty feelings that I was feeling, at least I wasn't drowning them away with alcohol this time. At least I was feeling things, handling them, and getting through them in a more positive way than in the past.

Feeling things strengthened me as a person again. It showed me that no matter how low I got or how bad things felt, there was always going to be a new day. It was always going to get better. There was only one way to go from the low places, and that was up. It showed me that no matter how bad I felt, I could handle it and I could get through it. I had the power within me to get through anything. It actually made me feel stronger than I ever had before when I was able to really feel all of the bad things but know that I could get through it, too. It made me feel alive, powerful, and resilient.

What I've found to work best for me when these types of days happen is to just accept it. Take it for what it is and let it happen. Let it all happen. Stop trying to deny and fight these undesirable days and just let them run their course. Let all the bad feelings in knowing that they won't last forever. I would put on my metaphorical battle gear and just bunker down for the emotional war I was on the foregrounds of.

When I started to do this, I felt less anxious about those bad feelings and found that they passed much quicker. I found that they didn't interrupt my life as much. I started to really listen to my body and my mind in a way. I would take a moment to really open up to what I was feeling and think, "Okay, it's just gonna be one of those days…" I fully acknowledged that that particular day might suck, but it wasn't going to be forever. I just had to get through it.

When I just accepted it and stopped fighting it, the whole situation would immediately feel lighter. It was like I finally wrapped my mind around the idea that it's okay to have an off day. It's okay to have a bad day. It's okay to feel like you're stuck in a funk. It's okay to not always be on your A-game. It's okay to not always be perfect and the happiest person in the world with the sun shining out of your *ss. We're allowed to have a bad day. We're allowed to have a day where sh*t just isn't all sunshine, rainbows, and butterflies.

I had a Monday recently where I had myself hyped up to just crush all of the things I wanted to get done. I was going to wake up early and get a workout in before my lash fill appointment. I was going to come home, have some lunch, and then dive into cleaning the entire house. I also planned on doing a sh*t ton of writing while I'm aiming to finish writing the first draft of this book. Well, guess what happened on that Monday? Not the plan. Not at all.

I got up and worked out on that day and I definitely went to get my lashes filled, because #priorities. But I got home and just fell off the band wagon for a few hours. It was a cold and rainy day and I ended up wasting a good hour or two on social media. I decided to try to start writing and barely got through one chapter before feeling like it was becoming forced and not from the heart. And guess what else? I didn't clean a DAMN thing. I felt anxiety creeping in. I just felt off. Something just wasn't flowing the way I had wanted it to on that day. I felt drained. I felt tired.

But here's the thing, I let it happen. I stopped stressing about what I hadn't accomplished. I let the anxiety kick in and told myself that it was time to just take care of myself instead. I told myself I wouldn't feel guilty about not accomplishing all of the things I had wanted to do. Those things could get done tomorrow and it wouldn't be the end of the world. I made myself some dinner and decided to watch a movie that I've been wanting to see for a few weeks instead. I totally relaxed and stopped thinking about all of the things I hadn't gotten done because of my off day and the funk I was feeling. Then I went to bed early. I could tell I was feeling super anxious and a little frazzled, and I didn't try to deny it or fight it. I let it happen and took care of myself instead.

What I've learned is super crucial is to not be too hard on yourself because of these days. Don't attack yourself for things not going the way you planned on them going. That's just life. Things happen and our plans get thrown off and redirected sometimes. It's not the end of the world. Just accept the fact that it's one of those days. It's a total off day. Accept it. Own it. Take care of yourself as needed. Let it pass. There's always tomorrow.

I want to stress a little bit more how crucial it is to take care of yourself on these days. Obviously we give ourselves our survival needs daily like food, water, and bathing...but this kind of taking care of ourselves is just as important, if not more important.

Sometimes the sh*t we go through emotionally requires more self-care than normal. It really demands that we step up and ask ourselves, "What do you need today, love?" Since some of us might not have someone else in our life that will step up and do this for us, some of us will have to do it for ourselves. But whether you have someone or not, learning to be able to do this is crucial. Take care of yourself, girl, you need it.

Tomorrow is another day and you've just got to get through this one. This mantra is golden. Use it daily. This is something I've told myself SO many times in the past few years. Whether it was surrounding my sobriety, my work, or my personal life, knowing this idea and repeating to myself often has been extremely helpful. Know that today is the only thing you need to worry about right now, and tomorrow will be here tomorrow. A new day. A new chance to figure it all out. Another day to get it all done. But don't worry about tomorrow until tomorrow comes. AMEN!

Give yourself some grace when it comes to having an off day. When you slip into a funk, take care of yourself rather than attacking yourself. Take full advantage of basking in the bad day. I'm talking self-care. I'm talking treating yourself. I'm talking listen to what your body is telling you.

Take a bubble bath. Eat something yummy. Meditate. Relax. Go easy on yourself. Don't obsess and harbor negative feelings about it. We are gentle, delicate women inside and we need to treat ourselves like that when things are going wrong or don't feel good.

I've learned in the last few years that it's just okay to have a bad day, an off day, a day where you are just in a complete and total funk. I've learned that some days I'm a bad*ss, and other days I'm a basket case. And there is nothing wrong with that. You don't have to be Beyonce every single day of your life. And if we're being totally real here, I bet Beyonce doesn't even feel like Beyonce every single day of her life. Unfortunately, I couldn't reach her for a comment about it for my book. #daretodream

Tomorrow is always a new day and we only have to focus on what's happening today. It's helped me so much to realize and accept all of the ideas surrounding this one. It's allowed me to stop constantly pushing myself. It's allowed me to give myself a little bit more grace. It's allowed me to stop holding myself up to such high standards regardless of what I was feeling in my life and in my heart.

Be gentle with yourself. Give yourself grace when you don't feel 100%. Don't worry about the things that derail your plans so much. Sometimes it's just the Universe telling you to slow down and focus on you. Sometimes it's something derailing us for a reason or for a bigger purpose. Maybe we just needed these day to stop, rewrite, and refresh.

Let the bad days, the off days, and the funk days happen. And remember that they will always pass and that you always have tomorrow to start a new day. We don't need to be on and perfect 100% of the time like we sometimes convince ourselves we need to be. Remember that.

THING #19 | YOUR BIGGEST DISAPPOINTMENTS WILL BE YOUR MOST VALUABLE TEACHERS

Ya'll...this is one of the biggest truth bombs you'll read in this book. This one is covered in gold, put up on a pedestal, and it should be reread about thirteen times. It's so f*cking powerful to wrap your head around and understand that it's actually mind blowing to me at times. This one takes time to see. Sometimes it doesn't happen right away. But I can promise you that in any situation this one will always be true one day. It might take a little while. It might not make sense for a long, long time. But I promise you that this is one of the biggest things I've learned so far in the thirty years I've had here on this Earth...That at some point, in some way, the biggest disappointments in your life will end up being your MOST valuable teachers.

There have been so many times in my life that things just didn't work out. Something went wrong. Something failed. Something I really wanted didn't end up being mine. Someone I really loved didn't love me anymore. I didn't get the job. I lost the best friend. I couldn't be successful at something I really wanted to succeed at. I literally almost lost my life because of my problems with alcohol and drugs... So many "mistakes." So many "failures." SO many times things just did not go the way I thought they should have.

All of these things were the biggest disappointments when they happened. I felt crushed. I was heartbroken. I felt like I was destined for sh*t. I felt like I couldn't catch a damn break. I kept asking WHY? Why did these things have to happen? WHY ME? What did I do to deserve this? Why couldn't this just work out for me this one time? Why didn't the things I prayed for ever get delivered to me? WHY? WHY? WHY? I got depressed. I got angry. I complained. I cried. I lost faith. You get the picture.

I could have never seen it in the moment, but it is SO clear to me now looking back that every single big disappointment in my life has been a situation that taught me something priceless. Each disappointment taught me something I couldn't learn in school. Each one taught me something that I couldn't buy a book about, or download a podcast about, or ask my mom about.

Somewhere down the road it would hit me. I'd have that big "AH-HA!" moment and it would come together and make complete sense. I would connect the dots of why that disappointment had to happen. The stars would align and the world would make sense again. That is when my disappointments became the most valuable teachers I could have ever looked for in my life.

Sometimes when it finally hit me it would be like a total mindf*ck situation. My jaw would literally drop. I would get goosebumps on my skin as sometimes they would be so clear that it would have me in utter disbelief. Somehow, someway it would always become crystal clear to me why something happened the way it did. It would become so obvious that this had to happen for me to learn something from it. Or it had to happen so that something else could happen afterwards.

There was always a lesson, a truth, and so much knowledge to be gained from what I thought had gone wrong. Something I would have never learned had I not gone through that disappointment first.

I would be shown that whatever that thing was, it couldn't happen because this thing was supposed to happen instead for me to learn something from it or be redirected by it. That sounded like a totally confusing sentence, but let me elaborate.

There was a bigger, grander plan beyond what I could ever see at the time for my life. There was a reason for exactly why things happened the way that they did in my life. It was a bigger picture of my journey and my purpose that required certain disappointments and redirections. It was all a part of the bigger journey and a part of the plan. The letdowns and disappointments had to happen. There was always something that I was intended to learn, see, realize, or pivot from from every single one of them that I faced.

Sometimes these were small things. Simple little things like something going wrong on one of my websites. I would get so frazzled and stressed over something like that, and then it would teach me by making me realize how much I relied on my success and online work to influence my mood. Something like being stopped for fifteen minutes at a train seemed like the most annoying delay in my day, but maybe it was keeping me from being in the wrong place at the wrong time. Maybe I missed a car accident. You never know.

It could be something else small like plans that I was really excited about getting cancelled. Soon enough I would realize that there was some reason I wasn't meant to be there or something else that needed my attention more. Situations like that would teach me to let things happen how they happen, because they always play out just as they should.

My biggest disappointments were the ones that taught me the realest things about life. They forced me to go through things. To feel things. To work through messy situations. To realize when things weren't good for me. They taught me to grow up. They taught me that some things just weren't meant to be. They taught me that no matter how hard I tried, some things were never going to work. It was a hard pill to swallow and a rude awakening back then, but now it makes SO much more sense.

When I think back on every terrible heartbreak I went through, I realize now that it was for the purpose of teaching me something to take with me moving forward. The heartbreaks would teach me that I needed to reevaluate who I let into my life. They would teach me what I needed to look for in a partner. They would teach me what I did not want from a partner and what I would not accept or allow into my life moving forward. They taught me to have higher standards. They taught me to hold out for someone that truly loved and cared about me.

They also taught me just how strong I was. They taught me that I could be okay on my own. They taught me that I could go through rough times and be okay. They taught me that sometimes I would even come out of them grateful. Grateful that all of those disappointments along the way taught me what I needed from someone else to be in a healthy and happy relationship.

When I think about the disappointments in my life regarding my career, it's so clear to me what I needed to learn. When I got laid off as a teacher, when I got kicked out of my student teaching program in college for something I posted on Facebook, when I didn't get the first promotion I went for…All those disappointments were teaching me that maybe that wasn't the path meant for me. Those disappointments taught me to be open to the idea of change. It made me more comfortable with the idea of trying out something different. It taught me that I could chase after my dreams on the side when I felt lost in what I was doing 9-5. I realized what a good thing it could be to take risks and try something new. It led to me creating and building my dream career that I am blessed enough to have today.

I can think back on many times in my life that something happened that felt absolutely Earth-shattering. I can remember how upset I would be. I can remember crying and hurting and wondering WHY this had to happen. But what I learned time and time again is that everything happens for some bigger reason that we can't always see or understand right away. You can't stop it, you can't change it, and it's got to just happen as it should.

What I learned to do is to start looking for what I could take away from whatever had happened to learn and grow moving forward. What was this supposed to teach me? What was this supposed to pull me away from? What could this be redirecting me towards? What is this putting right in front of my face for me to see and understand? These are the questions I started to ask myself instead.

I started to look for the purpose of what I was supposed to get out of these disappointments. I would start to ask myself, "Why is this happening FOR me, not TO me?" Sure enough, I could always find it somewhere down the road. It might not have been right away, but I always discovered it eventually.

Now as I've been calling them disappointments this whole time, I did realize at some point that maybe they didn't deserve that negative name so much. Maybe they deserved to be given a more meaningful, powerful name such as redirectors, wake-up calls, teachers, or eye-openers. Because in the big picture of things, that's exactly what all of those things did. The redirected me. They were wake up calls. They were great teachers. And boy, were they ever eye-openers!

Next time something happens that just sucks and has you super down, try to redirect your thoughts to this idea. Why is this happening FOR me? I started to do it daily and not only did it help me look for the lesson, it also helped me to not be effected so negatively by the things that didn't go the way I wanted them to. I started to look at whatever was going on and ask myself "Okay, what could this be trying to teach me? What could this be setting me up for? What could this show me?" Everything shifted with that more positive and optimistic mindset and approach to things.

Right now I'm currently fielding a big "disappointment" in regards to our upcoming wedding. We had originally planned to get engaged, run off quickly, and have a small but amazing destination wedding just five or six months later. I was SO excited. I was designing save the dates, browsing dresses online, and had created an entire Pinterest board full of inspo photos for my Mexican beach wedding. I was f*cking hype, ya'll.

After several weeks, things just weren't going smoothly. Something just didn't feel like it was flowing and happening as easily as it should have. People had already said they couldn't make it with such short notice. Paperwork would for some reason never go through in our emails. I couldn't put my finger on it but something just felt blocked. Something was keeping this from happening. My good old gut intuition was trying to speak to me, but I was way too excited about finding the perfect messy beach braid hairstyle to pin to my wedding Pinterest board to listen.

When we first decided to postpone the wedding for at least another year, I was crushed. I had been so excited and this felt like the biggest disappointment. I had a good ol' ugly cry about it. I let myself get super disappointed. I cried when I sent our wedding planner the email that we had decided to delay the wedding until later in the year at least. For a solid day I was moody and upset about having to delay everything and not have my exciting dream wedding to look forward to so soon.

So what did this one teach me? As I sit here right now I can tell you that it taught me to slow down. It taught me that there is no rush and another year isn't going to be the end of the world. I was so excited and hyped up that I was willing to not have any sort of planned out engagement party, wedding shower, bachelorette party, or anything like that. I was just rushing to squeeze in a wedding by a certain time.

This one also taught me to calm down and relax. It taught me that sometimes I can't do everything like buy a house, move, finish this book, and plan a destination wedding all at once. It taught me to take a f*cking chill pill and not get so upset about a redirection. It just wasn't meant to happen as soon as I thought it was going to. There's probably an even bigger reason that hasn't even hit me yet, but I'm sure I'll realize what it is at some point down the road.

What I've learned is that things we go through in life can teach us more than any book, podcast, college degree, or anything else ever could. Life experiences are the best teachers and the best eye-openers, and disappointments are some of the most impactful ones you will encounter.

I've learned to take disappointments with grace and know that they have a purpose. They have a good in them whether I see it right away or not. One day I always see the lesson. I always see the knowledge. I always see the good that I came to learn and be blessed with, no matter how big the disappointment may have once felt. It's all a part of a bigger plan and a bigger picture for our lives. We've just got to look for what life is teaching us along the way. It will always become crystal clear to us one day.

THING #20 | EVERY PERSON YOU MEET HAS A PURPOSE

There have been so many times in my life that I have met someone and not really thought twice about it. Just another person. Another acquaintance. It might have not seemed like much at first, but later it would be like a slap in the face awakening. Like HELLO, how did I not see this before? Sometimes it could be the most random encounter. Maybe I was waxing their eyebrows at the brow bar where I worked. Maybe we ended up being on a same flight that was delayed. Maybe it was someone I went out on a few dates with. Maybe it was someone that helped me carry my groceries…I can tell you from the bottom of my heart that most people I meet and spend even a short amount of time around I have met for a reason. It could be the most simple, basic fifteen-minute meeting…but it is absolutely for a reason. I believe that every single person that walks into a life walks into it for a reason and for a purpose, whether it may be big or small, good or bad.

The purpose of my meeting some people wasn't huge or life changing. Some of them didn't reroute the course of my life. Some of them were much more impactful. But every single one I can look at, take it for what its purpose might have been, and understand the reason behind that meeting. Even if it was just a quick interaction, I could see what that person might have been placed in my path for. Maybe it was to brighten my mood…Maybe it was to teach me a life lesson…but each one always for a certain purpose.

Retrospect can be a truly beautiful thing for this idea. Having the ability to look back on people and situations after they are over and have an actual understanding of them can be life changing. It's like you look back and finally it clicks and makes sense. You think, "Okay! THAT was why I needed to meet this person…"

The purpose might not be clear to you right away. It may even take YEARS of growth, maturity, and sometimes some healing to get there. But being open to there being a bigger meaning behind all of the encounters we have in our life just makes things make sense. It makes things fall into place. It teaches us. It gives purpose. It shows how it is all connected in the big picture of things.

Right before I got sober, I met a guy. Really the way we met is comical and so very typical of the old party animal version of myself that I used to be. I was driving to a girlfriend's apartment in downtown Detroit. I was dressed in a short, tight LBD (little black dress, duh), and was done up for a girls' night out. We were going to see a Magic Mike themed show with male dancers…yes please!

Cue the hottie riding on the motorcycle with the tattoos in front of me to turn around and make eye contact, and then turn around again to do a double take. I playfully waved before the light turned green because #YOLO. He turned around at the next street and began following me. We talked at the next red light and he got my number. I mean, was I really going to NOT give my number to the motorcycle riding, tatted up guy that just followed me to say hi? The baby blue eyes definitely didn't hurt his chances of getting my number either…

He met me and my girlfriends later that night at a skanky bar downtown and I sloppily suggested we get a shot. I was a real class act back then you guys, I know. I should have realized that he looked slightly out of place in a bar setting, but then he said the two words I NEVER expected to hear come out of his mouth, "I'm sober."

I remember the next day telling one of my girlfriends I wasn't sure if I wanted to continue seeing him after he kept in contact. I referred to him as "an addict" and said I didn't know if I wanted all of that baggage. Little did I know, I was about to face the music about the fact that I myself was an addict living in denial. But more on that later.

To fast forward through the middle part, we started seeing each other regularly. We started developing some kind of feelings for each other. Then the night I ended up in the Emergency Room from drinking and overdosing on pills happened. He had actually been coming to meet up with me that night, and obviously never found me because I had been in the ER unconscious and clearly didn't have my phone on me when he was calling to find out where I was. When I called him in tears the next morning just begging him to come see me he told me, "I can't be around someone like you."

That statement was like a dagger through the heart. HE, an actual addict, couldn't be around...ME!? What in the actual f*ck? The tables had totally turned. That was a huge wake up call. It was a huge slap in the face. I was so angry at him after he said it, but looking back I don't blame him one bit. I was still in quite a bit of denial about my issues with alcohol then. He was living in recovery and attending AA meetings regularly, while I was partying myself into the ER and almost dying. I don't blame him one bit for saying what he said on that morning. But the important part of this story is what happened next.

I told him that I had decided to be sober. I realized that almost losing my life was not something to be taken lightly and that I was given a second chance at life for a reason. I naively thought I was just going to keep doing what I had always done and just not drink. I was on the phone with him trying to convince him that I could still go out with my friends to the bars and be fine. He snapped back with "YOU CAN'T DO THAT."

Wake-up call from sober guy number two. The first should have been when he told me he couldn't be around someone like me. But I still didn't see it at the time. When he raised his voice to tell me that I couldn't keep just doing what I had always done it really messed with my head. I was still trying to be my typical invincible self and felt like I didn't need to listen to anyone else's advice or input. Something about the way he snapped at me must have clicked because after that phone conversation I remember sending him a text that maybe he was right...maybe I did need to start making more changes in my life if this was really going to work.

I knew deep down I had to make a change, but having a guy that might stick around if I made that change didn't hurt either. Things between us were actually good for a little while. He was there in my earliest sobriety days when I had no idea what I was doing. It became comforting to have someone to go on dates with sober. He already had gone through it so we related to each other on every level. In a way, he was a pseudo sponsor of sorts. I didn't attend AA or have a sponsor, but he became that person for me. I could always call him and he always listened when I had to talk about things.

Our situation ended up getting super messy down the road. We shared some more time together but ultimately feelings on both ends got messy and misconstrued. But there is one thing I will always say about that guy...He was placed there in my life EXACTLY when I needed him to be.

He wasn't just conveniently there right when I almost lost my life and decided to get sober. He was meant to be there. He was there in my first sober days. He kept me in check. He became the only person around that I could relate to. He was one of the only people that "got it" for a long time for me. I like to think that it's not just a coincidence that I met a sober guy right before and during the beginning of my sobriety. I don't believe in things happening by coincidence, I believe in things happening for a purpose. That involves the people that happen to come into our lives, too.

He was a part of my life not only when I first got sober, but he came back around a few more times when I needed him again. I'm talking came over no questions asked the day after my biggest heartbreak I mentioned earlier in this book. He came over, asked what happened, let me talk, let me cry…Then he was just there for me. He didn't try to be slick and get some while I was vulnerable. It wasn't about a hook up or anything like that. I remember he just held me and slept over. He was just there in a time when I felt alone and broken. He didn't even care that I texted him the day after my relationship ended. He showed up just like he always did before.

Like I said, feelings got messy and we didn't exactly end on the greatest terms, but looking back I will forever be grateful for him. I definitely loved this guy. Not in a "I want to get married and spend my life with you" kind of love…but a, "God and the Universe surely sent you to be my angel to guide me through the worst of times" kind of love. He was just there. Whenever I needed him. Whenever I was broken. He gave me hope. He had a purpose in my life. He came into it for a definite reason.

So my intention was not to dive deep into a past relationship of mine and another confusing love story for this chapter. My point was to show you that this guy was meant to be in my life for a purpose, but that he also was not meant to stay. He was not meant to always be a part of my life. He had a time and a purpose. He was not meant to be there forever. But rather he was delivered to come and serve his time and his purpose within my journey in life, and then go when he was done. Call it "woo-woo" or wacky to think about it that way, but I absolutely do. With every bone in my body and every piece of my soul.

I believe that I was meant to meet him the day that I did so that he would be in my life when I almost died. I believe that he was meant to be there so I had someone I could turn to in my first days of sobriety. I believe that he was my "sponsor" like the ones people have in AA programs. I believe he was there to give me support and guidance and a whole lot of hope. But I also believe that when his time was up and his job had been done, he would also be removed from my life. Although it hurt at the time, now I can see that he was never meant to stay. He was eventually no longer a part of my life at all, and we've never been in contact since.

There are many people from my past that I would ask myself WHY they were even a part of my life. A large amount of these people happen to be men. Maybe because I was young and a little boy crazy. Maybe because I was a serial dater just looking for real love. But I'm grateful that I can look back on most of them and point out their purpose. I can point out what they taught me, what they did for me, or what purpose they had in my life.

This really gets big when you can see the purpose of the people in your life that really hurt you. It can give you the ability to finally forgive. It can give you the opportunity to find closure. It can give you the chance to move on with your life. It can answer so many questions you might have still been left with. And it all can make SO much more sense when you're past it.

This didn't just happen in my life when it came to men. It happened with everyday encounters. Any person that walked into my life could leave a mark on it. They could leave the smallest little effect on me, but I know now that every single one is on purpose. It could be someone I randomly met at the grocery store or a gas station or at the airport waiting for a flight…Maybe just to brighten their day or vice versa. Maybe to walk away with some sort of new outlook on life. I know that nothing happens by chance or by coincidence. Everything happens for a true purpose and for a reason in our lives.

I've learned that anyone that came into to my life had a reason for being in it. Whether I saw it or not, they absolutely did. It gave me peace again after heartbreak to know this. It helped me appreciate the people in my life to know this. It made me cherish even the simplest interactions knowing this and believing this. It's incredible to know that whether good, bad, small, or big, every single person that walks into your life walks into it for a predetermined purpose. That every little interaction has a reason behind it.

Try to find the purpose and the reason behind everyone…and

always be grateful for your angels when they show up and serve their purpose. God, the Universe, and all of the Higher Powers out there send them for each and every one of us, exactly when we need them the most.

THING #21 | YOU DESERVE TO BE LOVED

I hope it doesn't take you ladies reading this as long as it took me to realize this one. Anyone that knows me personally for the past decade of my life can surely attest to the fact that this one took me a while to figure out. We've all dated that one person…The guy that we should have never spent as much time with as we did. Okay, the guy we probably should have never spent any time with AT ALL for that matter. You probably have that one person you can think of right away that you should have seen the red flags. The humongous red flags blowing in the tornado that would form from the whirlwind of chaos when sh*t really went downhill. You probably can think of that person right away. Well, I can think of at least a baker's dozen of those guys. I mean, sh*t, I could probably form a baseball team with those guys…and the opposing team…and the umpire, bat boys, and water boys…and maybe even fill up the front row ticket holders' seats as well.

Okay, so I MAY be exaggerating just a little bit, but you catch my drift here. I have a trail of *ssholes, douchebags, and sorry excuses for men in my past. Sometimes when I think about my dating life in my twenties, I feel like I should have been on some MTV reality show. My standards had gone out the window and I forgot how I deserved to be treated. The drama was real, and there was a LOT of it.

I was getting nasty emails from pissed off exes and playing stepmom to children WAY too soon in relationships. I was helping guys get their GED because they dropped out of school and lied to me about it. I was loaning money to guys and then calling them six months post break up STILL trying to get it paid back (like they promised). I was waking up finding Facebook messages about my boyfriend being "in the clear" because the blonde chick wanted to let him know she peed on a stick and she wasn't pregnant...ALL OF IT. AND MORE.

I'm telling you, guys, you don't know even know how it makes me feel to think that when I considered taking that one cheater back, he showed up at my door at 5am crying and I made him sleep on the floor at the foot on my bed like a dog... while my Chihuahua was curled up in fluffy blankets and sheets in bed with me. Okay, so that one still makes me laugh and gives me a little bit of petty satisfaction. If you've never made a sh*tty guy sleep on the floor at the foot of your bed like a dog before, have you really even lived?

Back to the point though. At what moment in our lives did we, as women, decide that it was okay to be treated like absolute sh*t? At what point did we make the choice that it was okay to get anything less than everything we deserve from a significant other? At what point did we forget that we should be treated with respect, compassion, and the most authentic, pure form of love? When did we get to this point where we forgot that WE DESERVE TO BE LOVED?

I know that looking back I feel like I forgot that I deserved to be loved at some point. Call it trust issues, call it daddy issues, call it whatever issues you'd like, but at some point I lowered my standards. I never made a conscious decision to say, "Starting today I want to find the saddest excuse for a man out there and make him all mine…" but at some point in time I decided to accept less than what I knew I deserved and wanted deep down in my heart. Why? Because I just wanted to feel loved and to not be alone.

I think that as women a lot of us fall into this trap at some point in our lives. We want a partner in crime. We want a date to all the weddings that come up in our twenties. We want someone to cuddle and watch Netflix with. We don't want to be alone forever, we want love. It's human nature to want this. We are programmed to search out others to be with and to share our life with.

The problem is that we fixate on needing to find someone to be happy. We get this idea in our heads that once we meet Mr. or Mrs. Right, things will just fall magically into place and make sense in our lives. Sometimes we become so desperate for this type of love that we start to compromise what we deserve in return just at the chance that we might be able to find someone. We want to feel loved so badly that we will sacrifice what we want from our partner just to have someone there. To quell our loneliness. To hold our hand. To sleep next to us at night.

When I was in my early twenties, I was not choosing the right men AT ALL. But I will say that my alcoholic self had a very "take no sh*t" attitude when it came to men. This made it very easy for me to kick them to the curb when they messed up. So I ran through a lot of sh*tty men rather quickly in my early twenties. I mean, I was still picking not-so-great guys, but at least I was smart enough to cut them off when they did something that wasn't okay according to my standards. I was f*cking ruthless with men back then, and sometimes I think I even got off on doing it.

The problem was that as I got older I started to lose that "boy bye" attitude. I began to let things slide because I was getting older and wanted to be with someone. My standards began to lower, my loneliness got louder, and I just wanted to find someone.

My sobriety was the first thing that really f*cked up my standards with men. In the beginning I was so lost, so lonely, and so uncomfortable that I just wanted to have someone around. I'd overlook all of the red flags and all of the drama just to have someone there during my dark days. This was the time period when I actually took back a cheater for a hot minute. He was so manipulative and I was so lost in my early sobriety struggle that I took him back just to have someone around that made me feel loved again.

Think about how f*cked up that is... I took back someone who slept with another women and could have possibly gotten her pregnant (I learned from that Facebook message) because I thought that he loved me. I thought that HE LOVED ME. I thought a man that could sleep with another woman and lie straight to my face about it even when I was screaming and crying and forcing him to read the messages out loud to me actually LOVED me. I don't think that could possibly be any more f*cked up.

I was using every dating app out there to try to find the magical Mr. Right that would solve all of my problems and make all of my dreams come true. I thought that it would just make things better if I found him. I was swiping right on every promising guy I saw on those apps in hopes that this could finally be the one.

The first thing I want to make clear before I start bashing dating apps is that I know there are good people on them. Sure, you're definitely going to have to become skilled at weeding out the bad eggs on there, but isn't that the case with dating no matter how you do it? There's always going to be that one guy that poses as a total gentleman just to try to get into your pants after one date. There's going to be that guy "going through a divorce" that has no idea what the hell he is looking for (and is probably not ready for anything AT ALL yet). There's also going to be that guy that continues to send you ten messages a day when you haven't responded to a single one of them. They're all on those apps ladies, so get ready.

Funny enough, I actually met Andrew on one of those apps after I just about gave up on them. So I guess it's true that God, the Universe, and all those Higher Powers won't give you want you want until it's the right time for it. But we'll touch more on him later.

What I want you to understand about being loved are some very basic ideas. These are the ideas I had to remind myself constantly to get myself out of that swiping right, meeting douchebags phase in my life. Here's what those ideas are:

1   It shouldn't be hard.
2   Find someone who truly loves ALL of you.
3   If someone wants to be with you, they will be with you.
4   Nobody that loves you will INTENTIONALLY hurt you.

Number One: It shouldn't be hard.

I remember my mother telling me this one multiple times in my young adult life. I always thought that things being hard didn't mean they were bad. I mean, have you watched any chick flicks lately? Isn't every woman supposed to be involved in a love triangle where Ryan Gosling makes you a painting balcony on his beautiful Southern home like he always promised and then you have to decide between him and your handsome, successful fiancé after your mother hides 365 letters from you after you're forced to leave after your summer of love? Or shouldn't you find the man of your dreams when you leave your alcoholic, abusive police officer husband to run away on a bus to some cute coastal town where the ghost of Josh Duhamel's wife warns you that your ex has come to hunt you down and burn down their perfect little corner store and then Josh saves you at the last minute after you shoot your ex-husband while he's strangling you and then you live happy ever after together?

Okay, so I may have watched those movies like a thousand times each while single and looking. But here's the thing…my mother was right. Every relationship of my past was absolute CHAOS. There were so full of red flags and drama that I could have been on an episode of *Jerry Springer*. They were never anything close to easy. They were hard. They were really f*cking hard. They were confusing. They were full of drama. I was constantly questioning things. I was constantly in the dark left wondering. I found myself constantly having to fix things. I would tell myself that nobody is perfect (which is true), but that I could help them in some way. I wanted to be the one that made it work through all of the hard times and trials. It would be just like it was in the movies if I could do that, right?

Ladies, IT SHOULDN'T BE THAT HARD. Sure, there will be bumps in the road. There will be ends that need to be tied up. There will be fights. It won't be all rainbows and butterflies all the time. But it should never feel like WORK. It should never feel like something that has to be full of stress and worry and conflict all day, every single day.

Number 2: Find Someone Who Truly Loves ALL of You

I remember dating a guy briefly in my twenties that was clearly successful. Drove an expensive car, always had on flashy designer belts, you know the drill…I'll be the first to say, DO YOU, BOO. Be proud of that money. But here's what I didn't like: I felt like I constantly had to be "done" when we did anything. It was always flashy dinners and lots of hair gel on his part. He was looking like a damn underwear model on a centerfold even when we went to the local, laid back Mexican place to eat. Now there's nothing wrong with wanting to look nice, but I started to feel like I HAD to be dressed cute and in heels anytime we went anywhere. There was never any throw my hair up in a top knot with leggings on outings when it came to our short lived whatever it was. There were never any chill nights in with no makeup, sweatpants, and delivery pizza. Being a girl that loves sweatpants and pizza, I had my doubts pretty quickly with that one.

The point here is I felt like with this one I had to be done up and going out all the time. He never even made an effort to have low-key dates together at either of our places. It started to feel like a show almost. A "look at me and how good we look" to anyone that was around to watch and see us. I f*cking hated it. I hated feeling like he only wanted to be with me when I was done up and looking good. It made me feel like I had to be that way for him to see me. Um, no thank you.

Another time I really realized how important this idea of a guy truly loving all of you was with Andrew. He saw all of my bad sides during the first year we lived together. He saw me sick in bed with the flu, sweaty and vomiting my life away at the toilet for two days straight. He saw me basically hyperventilating in a panic attack the night we had our worst fight ever and I thought we could have actually been done. He saw me picking the boogers off of my nose ring (if you have a nose ring, you totally know how those can drive you INSANE). He saw me have complete and total emotional meltdowns on multiple occasions. He saw the pretty, the ugly, the crazy, and the highlight reel. He truly saw ALL sides of me.

I knew it was different with him because no matter how bad the fighting got, he always told me that he wasn't going anywhere. No matter how much of my crazy I let him see, he always told me that we'd figure it out because he wanted a life with me. At first I was like, "WOW, this guy must really be a saint..." when it would happen. But then I opened my eyes and realized that it wasn't totally insane to think that a guy would stick around through all of the bad, the crazy, and the ugly...it meant that he actually loved ALL of me.

Number 3: If Someone Wants to Be With You, They Will Be With You

This one has always been the harsh truth that a lot of people don't want to hear. But if you can be brutally honest with yourself here, this one will save you a whole lot of waiting, questioning, confusion, and heartbreak. The bottom line truth is that if someone wants to be with you, then they are going to be with you. If they want to talk to you, they're gonna talk to you. If they want to see you, they're gonna see you. Plain and simple.

It doesn't need to be this long, complicated thing we millennials tend to make it be. It could be this plain and simple, cut and dry. If someone truly wants to be with you, they're going to act in a way that shows it. There will be no playing games. There will be no waiting to text back. There will be no wondering what you two are. If they truly want to be with you, they're going to do exactly that…be with you.

I know we have all been guilty of getting strung along longer than we should have allowed it to happen. We've all been guilty of holding onto hope when we really shouldn't have. We've all been the one to make the effort, plan the dates, always be the one driving to their place, etc. But ladies, open your eyes. STOP TRYING to make it happen. Stop making excuses. Stop taking bullsh*t excuses as justification to stay. Stop waiting. If they want it to happen, they are going to make it happen. Period.

Number 4: Nobody that loves you will INTENTIONALLY hurt you

This one is for all the ladies out there allowing disrespect, abuse, manipulation, and lying. I don't know how much more blunt I can be about this one, so I'll just repeat it again in case you didn't hear me. NOBODY THAT LOVES YOU WILL INTENTIONALLY HURT YOU.

Someone that truly loves you, I'm talking deep down in their heart loves you, will NEVER want to cause you harm, pain, and tears. Someone that truly loves you would never want to hurt you in any way shape or form. Cheating, lying, manipulation, control, abuse, ALL of it…that is NOT love.

This one is for the woman that has held on way too long. This one is for the woman whose allowed herself to be drug through the mud. This one is for the woman holding onto the idea that he will change one day. That he didn't mean it. That he doesn't realize the power of his words. GO. That is my only advice to you.

I have been there and I have held on way too long. I have allowed someone to hurt me. I have allowed someone to disrespect me. I have allowed someone to cheat on me and then let them back in. I have broken down into tears while being intimate again with someone that had cheated on me because all I could think about was him being with someone else while he was with me telling me that he loved me.

I'm just going to repeat it one last time because I know that every woman knows that this one is true deep down in her heart. NOBODY THAT LOVES YOU WILL INTENTIONALLY HURT YOU…EVER. No if's, and's or but's. No excuses. No justifications. No f*cking exceptions.

You deserve to be loved. You deserve to find a love that it true. You deserve to find someone who will be your best friend, your partner, and your teammate in life. No drama. No bullsh*t. No confusion. No uncertainty. Wait for that person.

If there's one thing I learned about finding love, it's that I'm glad I waited. I'm glad I held out for someone who checked all of my boxes. I'm glad I held out for someone who made it easy to love again. I'm glad I held out until it just felt right.

By the time you read this book, Andrew and I we will probably be engaged with a pretty little ring on my finger that I will excitedly share on social media. We might already be dancing under the stars on the beach in Mexico with our closest friends and family celebrating a marriage. By the time you discover and read this I may be carrying my first child, or we may already be building our family in our beautiful home together….Andrew showed me all the ways I deserved to be loved again, and I'm so glad I waited for him. Wait for the one that shows you that you deserve to be loved, too. Wait for that person. They're out there looking for you. I promise.

THING #22 | YOU WON'T AGREE WITH EVERYONE'S OPINIONS OR BELIEFS, BUT YOU SHOULD ALWAYS HAVE YOUR OWN

As I write this portion of the book, I have a post on my Facebook and Instagram where I shared a pretty negative opinion of a shirt that was being sold by a major retailer that sells to and targets young women. The shirt was blatantly poking fun at drinking problems and you KNOW your girl here has a platform to speak on this type of thing. I just could not bite my tongue on this one. It made me feel sick when I saw it, so I had to vent. My entire purpose and passion is helping and empowering other women, many who do struggle with alcohol issues and addiction on all levels. Seeing a shirt like the one I posted about pokes fun at, glamorizes, and normalizes alcoholism, which is not appropriate when so many people out there are struggling just to stay alive because of it. Your girl had to stand up for this one.

So I wrote my post and spilled my mind. I also tagged the company and made the post public. Now I was absolutely prepared that my incredible female audience that follows me on social media would have my back here. And, boy, did they show up! So many supportive comments, so many shares, and SO many messages thanking me for speaking up about the issue. Women on the internet can be absolutely incredible. They don't even know you personally but will show up for you, have your back, and fight for you day in and day out. It's really truly inspiring. But then came the internet trolls…

I knew this would happen. I knew that I was opening the door to a whole lot of criticism, a whole lot of "You're wrong," comments, and people trying to be plain old mean. The internet and social media can be a dark, nasty place, people. Click on just about anything that's gone viral and you'll be able to find lots of negativity in just seconds. But hey, everyone is free to voice their opinion just as I did.

So there were lots of comments on my post that were not so nice. Many told me to "Get over it," and other things in not so polite ways. If I allowed these things to get to me, it would totally have me doubting myself and feeling like sh*t. It would ruin my day. If I believed what these people, these absolute strangers had to say about me it could absolutely cause me to doubt everything about myself and what it is I stand for. It could make me just delete the post altogether to stop any more of them from coming in. Out of sight, out of mind…right?

Now I'm at a place in life where I know not everyone will share my opinion about this particular issue and this particular shirt. People are absolutely free to feel however they feel. They are free to share their opinion and tell me that they think I'm wrong or that they actually love the shirt and will be buying it. That's just life. We have the freedom to feel however we feel and vocalize it however we choose to.

Here's what I learned as I round up on thirty about this one. EVERYONE has their own opinion. I have mine. Suzie has hers. Frank has his. You mother will have THE MOST of them, undoubtedly. She will also have absolutely no problem telling you what that opinion of hers is all day, every day.

Everyone is going to feel a certain way about things that is determined by a number of factors. It may be determined by their parents, their friends, their spouse, the media, society, or a combination of a million different things. We each have our own unique opinion on just about every single thing that happens in life. We build and create these opinions because of what we experience in life and how things make us feel.

I've noticed from time to time that as I grew up I automatically took on my parent's opinions on a lot of things. When you are little, you think your parents know everything and that there is no other answer. How could they possible be wrong? They are your parents. The ones that taught little you everything you know. They had to be right about all of it all along, right?

At some point in life you start to realize that maybe all the opinions you heard growing up weren't right. Maybe they once seemed correct to you, but now they don't fit who you are anymore.

That's one of the coolest parts about getting older...realizing that you have your own voice, your own opinion, your own beliefs. You realize at some point they don't have to be the same as your parent's were. They don't have to match your best friend's. You can stand up with an opinion completely different from everyone you know, and that's completely fine. It's actually quite empowering and liberating, if you ask me.

An idea that can be hard to swallow for some is that everyone is ALLOWED to have their own opinion. It does not have to go along with the one you have. You could think pineapple on pizza is f*cking delicious and Mary down the street could literally hate pineapple on pizza so much that she starts a petition and a movement about it. You're not right. Mary isn't wrong. We're all allowed to feel how we feel and say what we say when it comes to any opinion of ours.

Having different opinions is not wrong in any way. It's part of life. It's part of living in a world where we have the right to share any opinion we have in any way we chose.

The thing that some people just can't seem to wrap their head around is that other people do NOT have to agree with your opinion. There is no rule saying that everyone has to go along with what someone else says. People don't have to feel the same way as you. They don't have to share your beliefs. You probably won't agree with about half of the things people will say or do in their lifetime. But you know what? It doesn't really matter!

You won't always agree with everyone else. But that's just how life and the world work. It's important that we realize that that is absolutely okay. We'll survive. The world will still turn. Tomorrow will still come whether you agree with someone else's opinion or not.

There are so many areas where people get super passionate about their personal opinions. I mean, come on, there were literal RIOTS over who our current president is. Looting, raiding, thousands of people in the streets of every major city...over our president. Look at things like the Black Lives Matter protests. Look at the Women's March. These are all examples of people coming together over sharing powerful opinions about things happening in our world today.

When it doesn't involve violence or harm, I think seeing people come together to stand up for their beliefs is an incredible thing to witness. Seeing people come together today like they did for rights decades ago is exciting to see. It's moving to see people care about their opinions and beliefs so passionately that they travel to places to come together and show the power of their beliefs in numbers. I am with you guys in sprit, no doubt, for some of those marches and demonstrations.

We were not given the right to have our own opinions or beliefs to be quiet or small about them. We were given these rights, these freedoms of speech to exercise them. To share our passion. To come together over what we care about. To record podcasts about them. To write books and blog posts about them. To create documentaries sharing them. This is exactly why you should take advantage of having an opinion and a belief that might not match everyone else's...because people fought and sometimes even gave up their lives for us to have these rights as mothers, as women, as transgender individuals, as members of the LGBT community, as women of color, as young women in schools with violence...as ALL of these things.

Another point I want to make is that you, baby girl, should never EVER back down from your opinion just because someone else doesn't like it. Your thoughts, feelings, and opinions are real. They are valid. They are 100% yours. Nobody has the right to take that away from you. Just because someone else doesn't agree with your opinions doesn't mean that they are wrong. Just because they bother someone else doesn't mean you should change them.

You stay true to you. You stay true to what you feel in your heart and in your soul. Ruffle a few feathers. Don't quiet down. Stand strong in your opinion and your beliefs in life. Speak up about the things that are important to you. Voice your thoughts on the things that you don't agree with.

I've learned in life that opinions and beliefs are a very powerful thing. I've learned that we should always have our own opinions, and that we should always stand up for the things that we feel passionate about. Never sit down and feel the need to be quiet or small. Not only as people, but as women today, our voices are being heard more than ever. What this taught me is that in a time when we are being heard, being considered, being listened to...Use your voice. Share your opinion. Stand up for each and every one of your beliefs. Someone before you fought for you to have these rights, so stand up and use the hell outta them.

THING #23 | YOU CAN BE MORE THAN ONE "THING"

I used to tell myself that I couldn't be good at EVERYTHING I did...That just wasn't how it worked in the world. There had to be some sort of balance to make it even. There was no way I could be talented at multiple things. I had to have my one thing I was good at. My one path I was supposed to take. My one passion and my one career that would excel. My niche. My area of expertise, if you will. I couldn't be good at everything I tried to do. If we all were good at everything it would just be a mess of people doing everything perfect. Nobody has THAT many talents. That just wouldn't be fair. I mean, everyone has to suck at something, right? Girl, I had it all wrong. Let me explain.

Sure, there are things that I am terrible at doing like not getting distracted by small dogs in public, figuring out simple math equations, and going anywhere outside of a five-mile radius of my home without using the GPS on my phone. Theres always going to be sh*t that just isn't our strong suit. There's going to be some things that we just plain old suck at doing.

Everyone is different and some people will just be better at some things than others naturally. People will excel and do amazing in some areas of their life, while doing not so hot in the other ones. That's just life and I guess God and the Universe had to balance it out at least a little bit to make it a little more fair for everyone out there.

But what I had wrong about this idea is the thought that I couldn't be really, really good at more than one thing in life. I was wrong to think that I ever had to limit myself to just one "thing" in life. I mean, who told me that I had to pick just one thing and stick to it forever, anyways? I honestly don't know where I initially got that idea from, but it stuck with me for a hot minute in my teens and twenties.

I went to college because my parents told me I had to. Plain and simple. In their eyes you went to school, chose your "thing" you would do as a career, and then that's what you did. That's what my brother had done and that's what they expected me to do. That's what I expected myself to do in the beginning, honestly. But somewhere along the way I realized I didn't want to do the one "thing" I had originally thought I wanted to do.

I remember telling my parents that I wanted to quit teaching preschool and go to beauty school. They were not on board with my big idea to chase my dreams of being in the beauty industry. In their defense, they had saved and invested to help pay for my college education, and it was very important to them. I know they just wanted me to be stable and secure with a career, but I just wasn't feeling it already back then.

I felt stuck. I felt tied down. I felt held back. Was I supposed to do just this one thing, even if I didn't feel head over heels passionate about it? Was I supposed to do this one thing, even if there were other things that lit a fire in my heart and pulled me in much, much more?

This was the first time I tested pushing the boundaries of being more than one thing. I stayed in school at the University of Michigan taking night classes, took out a loan to enroll myself in beauty school full time during the week, and then worked as a receptionist at a hair salon and go-go danced at Detroit bars on the weekends for extra cash. I was definitely not just one "thing" anymore. I was doing multiple things that really didn't go together at all.

So…I was a go-go dancing, phone-answering, college student that was also in beauty school learning how to do a full head of highlights. It sounds like the most random combination of things, and it absolutely was. People looked at me like, "HUH?" when I told them that random combo of things I was doing in my mid-twenties. But I was rocking every single f*cking one of them. I was good at all of the things I was doing.

It was the first time I realized I could be more than one thing. I could do multiple things, and guess what? I could be good at ALL of them! I could kill it at more than one thing that I wanted to do. THE. POSSIBILITIES. BECAME. ENDLESS.

I became extremely passionate about discovering all the wildly different things that there were out there in the world for me. It was extremely liberating to think that I could do anything and be anything that I wanted. It was empowering to know that I could pick a whole bunch of things I wanted to do and be good at all of them at the same time.

Since then I have become a hairstylist, a makeup artist, an entrepreneur, a YouTube video personality and creator, a blogger, a podcaster, a motivational speaker, a self-published author, a mindset coach, and probably a lot of other things that I am forgetting I was along the way. Whenever I do podcast interviews the host always asks me to tell their audience about me and what I do. I literally have to list out all of the things I do and stop for a minute to make sure I didn't forget anything. Because your girl is doing ALL the things.

An idea that has become popular in the online space lately that I love to challenge is everyone telling you that you need to "niche down" to be successful. While I see how having a very focused, specific audience and topic of choice can be good from a business standpoint, I don't think it gives us as women the chance to really be the unique and individual people that we are born and created to be.

Nothing I have done has been "niched down" and I draw in women of all ages, race, and walks of life for that exact reason. Why limit ourselves to talking about and sharing just one thing? Why let ourselves be only one thing and show one part of who we are, when we can share ALL the things we are knowledgeable about, passionate about, and talented at doing?

The idea of being more than one thing always makes me think about the idea of reinvention. When I hear this word the first person that jumps into my brain is always Madonna, the queen of recreating herself as many, many things throughout her career. This woman went from a Michigan-born schoolgirl to a superstar, to *Desperately Seeking Susan*, to an iconic singer, to a vogue-posing supermodel, to a diamond wearing old Hollywood star, to an erotic music video star, to Evita, to a skincare designer, to about a million other things along the way. The woman literally became anything and everything you could possibly think of.

A modern day example of this type of reinvention is Lady Gaga. The woman is truly unstoppable. She's been a meat-wearing red carpet walker, a jazz singer, a pop singer, a songwriter, a dancer, a fearless fashion icon, an Emmy-award winning actress, a motivational speaker, a philanthropist, and she crushed it in the new *A Star Is Born* remake of a cult favorite classic movie. She's our modern day Madonna. Proving once again that we as women can be as many things as we want to be, and we can be amazing at ALL of those things.

When I look at my life right now and realize all of the things I've been or am now, it makes me wonder how many more things I'll be in my future...The sky is the limit when it comes to all of the things I can do or be in my life. But then again, I could always be a female astronaut for NASA someday, too. So I guess the sky really isn't the limit after all.

You and I can be ALL THE THINGS. As many things as we want to be! What will you choose!? I don't know about you guys, but once I realized I didn't have to give myself just one label, one job, and one "thing" that I did, it was like the whole world truly opened up for me. I craved to bust out of the mold I had been unknowingly settling myself into for so long. I have a feeling all of you ladies reading this will feel exactly the same if you haven't already figured this one out.

Just because you're a mom, that doesn't mean you can't be an actress, an entrepreneur, or a CEO too. Just because you're a senior citizen aged woman, that doesn't mean you can't be a fashion icon, a blogger, and a bad*ss grandma too. Take any random combination of wildly different things you can possibly think of, and it's possible for you to be ALL of those things at the same time.

It's like that saying about women being a "lady" on the streets and a "freak" in the sheets… It's a little bit raunchy, but whoever started that saying had the right idea behind it. Because you truly can be all of the things as a woman, no matter how opposing and different they might be. Even if it's something like a lady and a freak. Your possibilities are endless, girl! It's time you own 'em!

I realized that I could be anything and do anything and it changed everything about my outlook on life. I felt limitless, free, and capable of doing it all. So I'm doing all the things that I want to do right now. I'm being ALL the things I want to be. I even just added merch to my website, so now I'm an online store merchandiser as well! See what I mean? I get an idea for a new "thing" and I go after it. Some work out, some don't. But all of them have the possibility to be something I could be great at.

The important thing to remember is that we can all be and do ALL of the things. No limits. Nothing holding us back. So do ALL the things you wanna do, and be all the things you wanna be! Don't keep yourself inside of one label. Don't tell yourself you can't do that thing that sparks your interest because it is too different from what you're already doing. Be all the things. Do all the things. Period.

THING #24 | YOU CAN HAVE IT ALL, BUT YOU'LL BE OKAY IF YOU DON'T

I can remember a million times in my life before turning thirty where things seemed to be going too good. Too good to be true. Like TOO many things were working out for me. If too many areas of my life were going well, I would stop and think to myself, "Oh sh*t. Something is gonna crash and burn." I was convinced that something was about to go south. If my career and finances were going well, my love life was surely about to plummet into the depths of Hell. If I met a nice guy and had amazing experiences with my friends and family lately, I was bound to have a sh*tty month in my business and my finances. I couldn't possibly have it good in ALL areas of my life at once. That just didn't happen for normal everyday people like me.

Somewhere along the way when I was younger I got this f*cked up concept in my head that if everything was going TOO good, something HAD to go wrong. I was convinced that I couldn't have it all. There was no possible way that God, the Universe, or those Higher Powers out there could possibly allow that much goodness into one person's life at one time.

There had to be some bad to balance out all of the good, right? It just couldn't possibly be fair for someone to have that much good at once. The other shoe certainly had to drop at some point. That's what I had convinced myself. It was totally and completely ridiculous. Do y'all question my sanity growing up yet, because as I write this book I definitely do from time to time.

So whenever things were going too good in my life I was always bracing for impact. I was waiting for that other shoe to drop, and for it to drop fast. I had my helmet and elbow pads on standby for whatever was going to knock me on my *ss soon and onto the ground. I was waiting for the thing that was going to fall apart, crash and burn, or throw a major wrench into my life to balance out all of the good stuff going on.

Looking back now, sometimes I think I was almost looking for it in a way that crossed into self-sabotage. Like if I figured it out quickly, I could better prepare myself and bounce back from it. It wouldn't be such a shock if I was ready for it and expecting it to happen.

Focusing that much on looking for what was going to go wrong was just a magnet for negative vibes...And we all know that with the Law of Attraction you attract what you think about the most. So I was probably pulling those negative things into my life like a f*cking rodeo king pulls in cattle with his lasso when I did this.

Here's what I learned about this idea...it wasn't real. It was something I had been convinced and brainwashed to believe at a young age by the pessimists, the Debbie Downers of the world, and the people that were afraid to actually think that you could have ALL the good things happening in your life at once. The people that actually like to play the victim. The "woe is me" people of the world. The people that are just looking for something to go wrong so they can complain about it out loud for everyone to hear.

There's a whole lot of these people out there and you know what? They want to rain on your parade. Hell, they rain on their own parade most of the time. The funny part is…they have no proof that this idea is true that you can't have it all. Nobody can prove this idea at all. It's something we've made up in our own heads.

So in reality I don't have any proof that you CAN have it all either, but if you've got enough faith, enough optimism, and enough belief in good things happening to good people…that's all the proof you really need. So just for sh*ts and giggles, let's start thinking that way on the regular!

If you can believe that it's possible to bring all the good things into your life that you want and desire, then you have absolutely every bit of power necessary to make that actually happen. It's all about dreaming big and thinking that everything you want in life is attainable and within your reach. It's about believing that there's no limit keeping you from getting all of the things you want. It's all about shifting your mindset.

It's about blocking out the negativity, the self-doubt, and the limiting beliefs. The less you focus on them, the less power they have. And the less power they have, the less negativity there will be in your life. Voila.

I also want to talk about the practice of manifestation. It's directly related to the whole Law of Attraction thing as well, and it's super important. I'll be up front and honest, I used to think manifestation was too woo-woo and out there for me. It felt weird. I thought it was absolutely ridiculous that you could sit around thinking about getting rich and famous, and it would just happen overnight by "manifesting" it. No way, Jose. But I didn't really get the whole manifestation thing and how it worked back then. What really helped me get on board with the idea was understanding it better.

Manifestation is not, "I'm gonna think about five million dollars and it's going to magically fall onto my lap." That's not how it works. You don't think about money and then stacks on stacks of Benjamins simply fall from the sky and into a pile neatly stacked in front of you. That would be amazeballs…but not actually possible.

Manifestation is about thinking and visualizing about something that you want. But, it also requires you to take action as well. If you don't follow up your thoughts with action and intention, it won't work.

Once I figured this out, the whole manifestation pill became way easier for me to swallow. There's even been a few times I've been like, "Holy sh*t…did I just manifest that?" in my own life. It's about thinking about all the things you want to have in your life, believing that they are possible, and then taking action towards making them actually happen. Because, remember…we can have all of those things.

There is absolutely no reason we can't have it all. There is no rule saying we can only have a certain percentage of things that we want for ourselves and our life and once we reach that maximum percent, that's it. You don't max out the good things in your life like you do with the limit on your Victoria's Secret credit card. There's no limit to them. There's nothing stopping us from going after all of them. There's nothing stopping us from receiving all of them.

So while I'm going on and on about how you CAN have it all, I also want to play devil's advocate and flip this idea to the opposite side. What if some of the things you want to have just don't happen?

You might NOT have it all. There might just be some things you want that you won't ever have. Some things just aren't meant to be yours. There's two things I want to make very clear about this that I have learned along the way to make you ladies better understand this one from the other side as well:

1. Some things you just aren't meant to have.
2. You'll survive if you don't have it all.

Number One: Some things you just aren't meant to have.

Some things aren't meant to be a part of your life. The big plan for your life just doesn't include some of the things you think should be a part of it. This is NOT a bad thing. This is destiny. This is the Universe blocking the things not meant for you. This is God blocking out certain things so that he can make room for other things. These are things you didn't know you needed, but that you absolutely do need. This is your life's path taking shape. This is the Higher Powers making everything happen for a reason. I know this can be hard to accept, and it will definitely take a whole lot of trust to really grasp and understand it sometimes.

There are things that don't happen in our lives because something ELSE is supposed to happen instead. Something bigger and better. Something you didn't know you needed. Something you didn't know would make your life a whole lot better. Have faith and TRUST in this idea. There may be things you think you want or need to be happy, but you could have the whole thing wrong.

I've mentioned it previously in this book, but I feel like at some point down the road you always realize why something didn't work out the way you wanted it to. Whether it was a relationship, something with your career, or anything else, it always makes sense at some point. You can always see why once you are beyond it. You can understand that maybe it was just preparing you for something better that you were meant to have. You will finally realize one day that some things you will just never have and that there is a reason for that.

Number Two: You'll survive if you don't have it all.

Anyone that has lived a few years can probably understand this one pretty easily. When something doesn't go your way or something you thought you really wanted and needed doesn't happen for you, it can be frustrating. It can be a blow to your confidence. It can be a rainy day cloud over the sunny day you had imagined for yourself. BUT...tomorrow will always come. You will wake up to live another day. YOU'LL SURVIVE.

Just because things don't play out the way you want them to doesn't mean it's the end of the world. If everything doesn't go perfect in your life, you'll still be okay. Not having all the things you want is not a death sentence. There are going to be so many things that will go "wrong" or that you will "lose" in your life that you will lose count. There will be so many things you want that you won't get. That's just life.

It's important to see that not having it all can teach us things as well. Times of trial and times of failure or loss build us. They shape us. They mold us into unique human beings. They teach us resilience. If we had everything we wanted in life just handed to us, we would have no character. We would have no life experience. We wouldn't know how to bounce back and survive this thing called life if everything was always easy and handed to us on a silver platter.

When you look at things from this point of view, it's easier to see that we need to not just have everything handed to us that we want. We need to not have it all easily and neatly placed into our lives. We need to learn how to navigate not having things so easily. We need to learn how to figure things out when they don't go as planned. We need to learn how to work hard to get the things we desire. We need to learn that we are resilient and flexible beings that can adapt and change...and that we can still be okay even if we don't have it all.

I realized that it's great to have it all, and that its absolutely possible in each and every one of our lives. But I also learned that sometimes I just won't have it all. Sometimes I'm just not meant to have all the things I want for a reason bigger than me that I don't even understand or know. I'll survive. I'll see why someday.

But in the meantime, I'm standing here with open arms grateful and ready to take in all the good things I can. Because I realize that I can have all the good things that are meant to fill up my life. I can have a successful career, a wonderful relationship, a beautiful home, the cutest dog, priceless friendships, supportive family, and anything else I ever wanted in life. Bring it all on, Universe. Your girl is ready for all of it.

THING #25 | IT'S NEVER TOO LATE TO REWRITE YOUR STORY

Waking up in an Emergency Room hospital bed, I had no idea where I was. Honestly, I was still so f*cked up at that point when I opened my eyes that I only remember flashes of memories from it. I was trying to rip the IVs out of my arms and the multiple EKG sensors and wires off of my chest. I was trying to get out of the hospital bed I was in, absolutely freaking out. I had no clue what the f*ck was going on. The nurse ran over and tried to hold me down to the bed to keep me from moving. Why was I here, why was I alone, and WHAT THE F*CK just happened!? This wasn't the first time I'd been in a situation like this, but I decided shortly after being released to go home that it certainly would be the last time.

If you have read my first self-published book, *Sober as F****, then you may already know this story of mine all too well. If you're new to my books, allow me to take you on a little walk down memory lane...

I grew up desperate to be perfect, desperate to be loved, and desperate to be "enough." From a very young age when I was on stage doing ballet with a high bun, fluffy tutu, and perfectly applied red lipstick, I needed the attention and reassurance of others. I needed it to think that I was beautiful enough, that I was skinny enough, that I was smart enough, and that I myself was enough. If you really want to hear all the details about everything that led to my problems with alcohol and addiction, I highly suggest you read that book. For the sake of not repeating the entire thing here again, I'll shorten it to the cliff notes version for you ladies.

I was your typical "party girl" growing up. I was basically the Walmart version of Paris Hilton circa '05 with my half gallon of five o'clock vodka at every party, every weekend. It basically tastes like straight gasoline and rubbing alcohol blended together, if you haven't tried it yourself. I drank it straight from the bottle without a chaser and I thought it made me look like a bad*ss when really, it just made me look like a straight up alcoholic.

There I was every Saturday night with my short skirts, white girl clip-in weave, and the largest bottle of alcohol I could get for the least amount of money possible. SO CUTE.

The cocktail of my experiences from my teenage years and twenties, my past traumas, a sexual assault experience, a New Year's Eve laced drink that led to an ensuing rape, and a slew of horrible relationships with toxic men...Welcome to what I like to call my downward spiral, ladies and gentleman.

I had no intentions of ever dealing with any of my issues or any of the traumas that I experienced in life because it made me feel weak to admit that I was struggling. And you know that I hated to look anything other than perfect and envious to everyone that looked at me. So I drowned away every emotion, every memory, and every little thing that I didn't want to face or feel...one overflowing shot of cheap vodka at a time. As you can imagine, things got ugly.

I was blacked out drunk every time I drank. I drank every weekend, if not more often. I woke up not knowing where I was, who I was with, or what had happened most mornings. You can only imagine the situations I was getting myself into. All the time. I'm shocked sometimes that terrible things didn't happen to me more often than they did. And I'm always shocked that I didn't open my eyes and realize that TERRIBLE things were happening to me because of the way I was living my life at any point along the way. That was until May 25th 2015 happened...

I had drunk an ungodly amount of alcohol for my small 5-foot frame. We were going to a music festival in Downtown Detroit and I wanted to be smashed off my *ss drunk so that I could have a crazy, rager kind of night. To wrap things up for you guys, I consumed so much alcohol before even getting inside that I don't remember being there at all. I then took a handful of random pills from a stranger as he shoveled them into my open mouth.

I collapsed on the concrete and had to be carried to the front of the festival and then rushed to the Emergency Room strapped down in an ambulance. I had a small seizure and bit halfway into my tongue, and then my body began shutting down in response to the very large, lethal cocktail of tequila, vodka, hard lemonade, ecstasy, Molly, and ketamine that I had consumed in about an hour's time. Just to make that crystal clear for you all...Yes, ketamine is commonly found in animal tranquilizers including some that are used on horses. That's right, animals that can weigh upwards of 1,500 pounds versus my 115 pounds. Clearly I was annihilated.

After I was admitted to the hospital, my heart rate shot up so high that I had to be monitored to make sure I didn't go into full cardiac arrest. A doctor sat down at some point during my stay and told me that after the lethal overdose of drugs and alcohol I had taken, I shouldn't have been alive. He wasn't sure how my body pulled through after it was shutting down on itself, but somehow it did. I walked out of that hospital alive when I absolutely shouldn't have.

That night was enough to scare me straight. People were scared to death that I was dead. Seeing them cry... Seeing them hug me and thank God I was alive...I knew I could never put the people around me through something like that ever again. I knew I couldn't chance putting myself through something like that again and probably not make it out alive the next time. This wasn't just another crazy drunk story to tell, this was my rock bottom and my second chance.

I felt like the most pathetic, worthless human being on the planet as I sat sending out apology messages to everyone that was trying to find out if I was alive or not the night before. The biggest apology went to my mother, because she almost lost her daughter.

Nothing could have made me feel more lost, more broken, and more out of options than I felt after that night. And as a result of that night, I would never consume another drop of alcohol again...

The young woman I just told you this story about might sound like it couldn't possibly have been me. She is the exact opposite of everything that I am and everything that I stand for today. But, I was that girl...I was a drunk. I was an addict. I was a mess. I was narcissistic. I was manipulative. I was sleazy. I didn't care about anyone but myself. I hurt people. I hurt myself. I was lost. I was NOT a good person...at all.

When I look at myself today, just over three years sober as I write this book, I know that I am not that girl anymore. I honestly don't even know who she is anymore. She is an absolute and total stranger to me now.

I took the pieces of my life when it was completely shattered and rebuilt it into one that I am so grateful and humbled to live today. I am so grateful to be here and to still be alive that it could still bring me to tears on some days. I share all of this to tell you that I have rewritten EVERYTHING about my story, and you, girl, can do the exact same thing.

You can change everything today. Right now. This very second. It doesn't matter what you've done. It doesn't matter how many times you've screwed it all up. It doesn't matter how lost you feel at this very moment. It doesn't matter that you feel like an absolute piece of sh*t. You can take your situation, as f*cked up as it is, and change it.

You CAN still rewrite your story. STARTING. RIGHT. NOW. Make the choice. Make the decision. Right here and right now... What do you want to rewrite about your own story? I'll be the living, breathing example to you guys that you can take any sh*tty, difficult situation and turn it around.

I went from waking up trying to figure out where I was by the photos hanging on a stranger's kitchen refrigerator to coaching women on how to turn their lives into their best life possible. I went from passing out on my couch with my apartment door left wide open after a guy left, to writing a book about my journey of living happily ever after in sobriety. I went from hooking up with any sh*tty guy that gave me attention to preaching in a podcast episode about how to demand the proper treatment and respect from the men in your life. Still think you're hopeless and lost and could never come back from where you've been in the past? Try me.

What I realized along the way were some very important ideas about our "story." One big, huge idea I want all of you ladies reading this to know is that your story doesn't ever get set in stone unless you want it to. There is no finish line, no end point, and no destination where someone tells you that what you are at that moment is what you always have to be. There is no point were someone tells you that your life has to stay exactly as it is forever. Our story goes on and on and can change at any point as long as we want it to.

There is also no rule that we have to stay in any "story" we no longer want to be a part of. Of course, we don't want to intentionally harm or hurt anyone, so please keep that in mind. But what I'm referring to is that we can leave our story at any time if it doesn't fit anymore. If it just doesn't feel right, we have every single right to rewrite it into something that does. We can choose to change it right then and there. I'm not saying abandon your family and your children and be a free-roaming hippie for the rest of your life, but I am saying to rewrite your story in a different way if it's no longer working for you.

I was the "party girl" for a very long time. It was the only way of living that I knew back then. But that story no longer served me. It didn't work. I didn't fit into the story of my old life after getting sober either. The places didn't feel right anymore, the people didn't feel right anymore, and who I was didn't feel right anymore. So I followed my heart and I rewrote all of it. Every last detail.

Our story right now is not the story we have to keep forever. We are not stuck here. Our story can change and rewrite itself over and over again throughout our lives as we grow and change and evolve as women.

It's a bit liberating to think about really...That at any point in our life we can rewrite everything. We can stand up, say, "This isn't the story I want for myself" and change it all. We can rewrite it starting all the way back at page one at any given point. That idea is so full of hope, light, and possibility that it's truly unbelievable.

I learned that my past story did not define me. I learned that my current story doesn't have to be the one I stick with forever. And I also learned that I can rewrite anything about my story whenever I feel the need to. I had the power to rewrite it all along, I just didn't realize it for quite some time. But once I did realize I had that power over my own story, it was like "Watch out world!" I was ready to rewrite the whole damn thing. And that's exactly what I did.

I hope that you realize the same things I did. I hope you realize that we don't ever have to stay in the same story if it doesn't fit anymore. We have the power to take our story, put brand new blank pages in it, and rewrite it to be whatever we want it to be. We can rewrite the first edition, we can write the sequel, and we can even self-publish it and sell it on Amazon if we really want to...just like I did. Rewrite your story into one that you love. It is never impossible and it is NEVER too late. So tell me, what will your story be?

THING #26 | ACCEPTING HELP IS A GAME CHANGER

I have been my own worst enemy in the past when it came to admitting that I can't do something on my own. A lot of it definitely comes from my stubbornness and my hard headed attitude I've had for most of my life. I've never liked to admit that I can't do something. I don't like failure. I hate to ask someone else to do something that I think I should be able to do all by myself. And I've absolutely loathed asking for help my entire life because in my mind, I should be superwoman at all times and in all situations. I tended to always have that "I don't need a man; I can do it myself" attitude about most things...That is until it came to things like fixing my broken garbage disposal or killing significantly large spiders on my own.

We, as women, like to think that we are unstoppable. We love the idea that we can do anything a man can do on our own just as good, if not better. (WOO HOO!) That's not just an idea ladies, it's a factual statement and don't you forget it!

We like to kill the game as a single mom raising bad*ss little humans. We like building our side business by putting in the entrepreneurial work. We love being able to support ourselves financially with our income. We like to juggle it all on our own with superhuman strength. We definitely don't need help juggling the five thousand responsibilities in our lives, right? Wrong.

Now, don't get me wrong, it's an awesome thing to be an independent, empowered, and strong woman in the world today. Anyone that knows me knows that I will stand up on my soapbox and preach about how women today can do ANYTHING they want, and do it well. The things we can do are limitless. A lot of them we can do on our own, no help needed. But sometimes we just can't do all the things we want to do completely on our own.

Sometimes we just need a little bit of help. Whether its financially, physically, mentally, or emotionally...we all can use a helping hand sometimes in life.

Asking for and accepting help is not a bad thing. For some reason some of us associate needing help as weak or failing. We see it as an age old damsel in distress stereotype. This is exactly what I did for quite some time. I always thought that asking for help was a bad thing. I thought it meant I wasn't strong or couldn't do things on my own. Ya'll know your girl was bound and determined to be stubborn as hell and try to do it all alone, especially when it came to my getting sober.

We've touched on my journey in sobriety a bit in this book, but I haven't covered some of the darker times that happened in the middle of it. The truth is, even though it might seem like it was easy for me on the outside when you look at my books, my podcast, and everything I've been able to do...it was actually the farthest thing from easy for me.

I struggled so much during my first two years sober. I battled with intense episodes of anxiety and depression. I lost all sense of myself and what I deserved from men in my life. I withdrew from a lot of my friends and even my family for a while. I didn't know how to be okay during that time. I had no idea who I was anymore. I had taken everything out of my life that was familiar. It was a very dark and trying time in my life.

I never realized just how much of a challenge sobriety was going to be for me on an emotional and mental level. I knew it would be hard sometimes to block out the urges to drink, but I was in no way prepared for everything else that I would have to face. The emotional rollercoaster was just that, a complete f*cking rollercoaster of ups and downs on a daily basis. I would cry out of nowhere. I would lash out at people. I would get depressed. I would be super happy. I was all over the place.

Sobriety forced me to look at myself on a deeper level mentally. It shone a light on the things I didn't like about myself. It reminded me of traumas and scarring experiences from my past. It made me relive and feel things I never wanted to think about and relive ever again. Getting sober made me finally face and deal with ALL of my own sh*t. The sh*t that I had been drowning away with alcohol for years.

Being the stubborn, hard-headed girl that I am, I told myself that I didn't need anyone else or anyone's help to get through it. I was strong. I had will power. I said no to therapy. I said no to AA. I said no to anyone that questioned my ability to do it on my own. I mean, if I had gotten this far without ever having a relapse that had to mean that I had enough willpower to get through it all by myself, right? I was being naive and had convinced myself to have a false sense of confidence about something I really knew nothing about. Big surprise…I was completely and totally wrong.

The first time I finally decided I needed help was about six months into my sobriety. I was an emotional wreck. I knew if I didn't get help in some way that I was going to lose my mind. I finally accepted the idea that maybe it would be easier if I let someone else in. Maybe it would be easier if I accepted some sort of help. I wasn't sure exactly what I needed, but I was willing to at least be open to it for the first time in my sobriety. I finally considered that maybe help wasn't such a bad thing after all.

The first place I looked for help was at the church I used to attend. It was an absolute game changer. I felt a sense of community, support, and love when I first started going there. It started to help.

I felt like I was a part of something bigger. I felt meaning to my life like I never had before. It made me feel supported when complete strangers from the church checked in on me. I realized that other people out there cared and wanted to help me. Not for any ulterior motive, but just because they were good people. I went to church every single weekend by myself. I sang. I prayed. Sometimes I even cried. But I felt the battle get just a little bit easier during that time.

The next way I opened myself up to accepting help was finally finding a therapist. I had been throwing around the idea of going to therapy from day one of my sobriety, but I never actually followed through with it. I had never even looked into finding someone to see at all. I think for a while I just said I wanted to find a therapist because it sounded like it was what I should have been saying at that time. I knew it was what others wanted to hear, and in some f*cked up way saying it out loud almost made me fool myself into thinking I was actually open to it too.

I didn't start seeing my therapist until after I was a whole year sober. Don't even ask me how I made it to a year without relapsing, because I couldn't even give you an answer to that one. I'm honestly shocked that I made it that long myself. But after a year of fighting and being stubborn on my own, I was ready to let help in. I was falling apart. I was struggling so badly and was in such a bad place that I finally gave in. I found a therapist and scheduled my first appointment.

I sat on that couch, tissues in hand, and sobbed through my entire first appointment. I ugly-cried for an hour straight. I didn't even wear makeup because I knew it was going to be waterworks central. My mom drove me there because she knew I was going to be super emotional after that first appointment. Bless her heart. During that first appointment I word vomited out every single thing that had happened. I replayed my past, my struggles with alcohol, and what a lost, confused, broken place I was in at that moment. I let everything out.

From that first day to today, therapy was the biggest help and biggest game changer to me. I'm not sure why I was so opposed to it for as long as I was, but it truly changed everything once I accepted the help. Therapy has been my most powerful lifeline when it came to getting though sobriety, depression, anxiety, relationships, trauma, figuring out myself and everything else in between. Now on the other end of things, I only wish I had been open to accepting it sooner.

If I had accepted the help that therapy had to offer me earlier on, I often wonder if sobriety would have been a lot easier for me. I wonder if I would have struggled as much as I did. I wonder if I would have healed faster. I wonder if I would have understood my alcohol abuse better from the beginning. There are so many things that I think therapy would have changed early on, had I just been accepting of it.

I had to figure it out the hard way, but it doesn't have to be that way for everyone. You don't always have to do it alone. You don't have to do it without help. You don't always have to be superwoman. You don't have to pretend that everything is okay and that you have it under control when you don't.

It's okay to say, "HEY! I need help!" It's okay to admit that you need support. It's okay to say that you were wrong and you can't do it all on your own. It's okay to wave that white flag up in the air sometimes and surrender.

Accept the help. Accept all of the help that is available out there for you. Be open to it all. Whether you struggle with an addiction like I did or not, help is available to us in so many ways in our lives. Let the grandparents take the kids for a night. Let your partner be someone you can lean on. Let your friends prepare you a home cooked meal when your life is in a state of chaos.

Once we can get past the idea that accepting help is a bad thing, we can utilize and take advantage of it. We can use it to live a better life. We can use it to get to where we need to be. We can use it to get a little bit of the weight of the world off of our shoulders. We can use it to not absolutely lose our f*cking minds sometimes.

People are there for you more than you even realize. People love you and care about you and want what is best for you in life. You would be shocked at how many people will come forward to help when you need it most. Your friends, your family, and sometimes even complete strangers will show up for you with an outstretched helping hand. It's not so crazy to think that people out there have good hearts and will be there when your life is not in its prettiest state. Be open to it. Be accepting of it. It can make things so much easier.

What I learned is that accepting help doesn't make me weak or a failure. It means I'm aware that sometimes I don't have to be superwoman. I can accept the help others offer me. Accepting help is me knowing that I can't do it alone sometimes and finally being okay with that idea.

Realizing how much help there is available to us and seeing how many people want to help you is heart-warming and inspiring. There are so many amazing and compassionate people that will step up and help when you need it. It showed me that I am not alone in this, and that I never was. There have always been people that were offering help, I just had to be open to it.

I love knowing that today with my books, podcast, coaching, and content, I can provide that same help to someone else. I love knowing that after realizing just how much accepting help made me successful in my own journey, I can do that for someone else now too. It has been such a beautiful journey in my own life to start accepting help and seeing how much it did for me. I can't wait to continue watching how I can help others grow in that same way. I hope to show so many more women that's it's okay to ask for help. It's okay to ask for it. It's okay to take it. It's okay to use it.

THING #27 | THE OLDER YOU GET, THE MORE YOU'LL BE ABLE TO CALL YOUR OWN SH*T OUT

When we are young we tend to think that we are invincible, that we are always right, and that everyone else is just wrong. I think we can all attest to this one. Teenagers are just little *ssholes sometimes. Girls in their twenties are sometimes just as bad, if not worse. We're young and stubborn and we don't like to acknowledge the things that we might be wrong about. We don't like to acknowledge when we are the ones that f*cked up. We don't like to admit that we made the big mistakes. We don't like to take the blame. We don't like to call ourselves out on our own sh*t. It's much easier to point a finger, blame someone else, or just make excuses to defend ourselves instead. Plain and simple.

At some point this changed for me quite a bit. I'm well aware that it might not happen for everyone this way, and that some people will never want to man up and own it when they are in the wrong. Some people will never get to a point of maturity and logical thinking where they can look at themselves and do this. Some people will just always be *ssholes. But a lot of us will outgrow that stage of our lives eventually. I'd like to think that I'm getting there. It may have only took me thirty years to get there, but at least I'm getting there.

The older I get, the more and more I notice that I am highly aware of my own sh*t. Maybe it's from more life experiences, more maturity, and being more logical with ourselves, but I am able to call my own sh*t out like a pro nowadays.

I can look at myself in a much more objective manner now and call myself out when I'm wrong. I can call out the things I've done that are things I struggle with. I can recognize when my response to a situation or a person isn't one that I should be proud of. I can tell myself to stop being such a b*tch in a situation. I can remind myself to chill the f*ck out. I can also call myself out when I'm being petty. I've become the master of being able to catch myself in the act when I'm doing something that is not so pretty.

Being able to catch yourself in your not so pretty moments and reactions can be a total game changer. It's really a whole other level of elevated thinking that can show you a lot about who you are and who you've come to be in your life, and who you want to be in your life.

I can also call out how much I've picked up traits as an adult because of what I was around as a child or as a teenager. There are times that I stop myself and say, "OMG...you are being your mother right now" when I start nagging on Andrew. Most of us will somewhat become our mother one day. It's a blessing and a curse, people.

I literally found myself getting so annoyed one day that Andrew didn't want to eat the chicken stir fry I made for dinner. Didn't he realize that I SLAVED over the stove to make him a home cooked meal!? What an unappreciative d*ck. For one brief moment, I said in my own head, "Well if he doesn't appreciate all of my hard work then I just won't cook dinner for him anymore..." But then I caught myself. That was something my mother would have said when I was being picky as a child, refusing to eat my Brussel sprouts. Calm down, Sarah. He just didn't like the stir fry sauce you bought. It's not the end of the world. And we all know that my overdramatic *ss still made dinner again the very next night, too.

Ask anyone who hates to admit that they are wrong during a fight with their significant other, it's not always fun being the one to admit that you are in the wrong. It can also be super difficult to cut through your own pride and call out your own sh*t during a heated argument. Nobody likes to admit that they overreacted, said something inappropriate, or that something was entirely their fault. That's how like 99% of fights in relationships happen, right?

I can honestly say that the older I get, the more well-versed I am at healthy communication during fights. I'm literally somehow able to give myself a moment, really process things, take a step back, and see things from all sides. When I was young? HELL NO. It was always the guy's fault. I was way too prideful and selfish to ever be able to handle things like that much of an adult back then. I was never the one in the wrong, duh.

With time and with more life under my belt, I've been able to really push my pride to the side and look at things from all angles. I'm able to play devil's advocate pretty damn good and see both sides of any argument or issue. I can even own my part in the fight and call myself out on what I did wrong. It may not always be easy to do so, but it is very possible. Just because I might not do it immediately doesn't mean I'm totally failing here. I'm just a work in progress.

I'll be up front and admit that I still react without thinking at times. Every once in a while, I'll word vomit something out that I wish I could scoop up and shove right back down my throat. You know, the type of statements that the minute the words leave your lips you think "WHY did I just say that!?" You wish you could rewind and put them back where they came from. But growing up has really expanded my tool belt when it comes to handling these situations.

I think the biggest area of life that I've really seen this one come full circle is in my relationship. Andrew and I fight, which is absolutely normal. We bicker about things that don't even matter. Sometimes over the DUMBEST sh*t ever. Regardless, that's part of a relationship. But, the longer we spend together and the more we started to really plan a future and a life together, we realized that we had to really work at making sure we fought in a healthy way. It sounds funny to call fighting healthy, but I think it is a balanced part of every relationship. It just happens, and you've got to be able to get through it as amicably as possible.

When we fight now I stop and take a minute to think, "Okay, what did I do here?" and most of the time it doesn't take me long to figure it out. Nine times out of ten it's something I said that was taken very personally. My tendency to be a verbal ninja in the middle of a fight does this sometimes. I say things and blurt them out without thinking, and sometimes they are mean things. I might have not intended for them to be so mean, but I also know that I can't control how other people feel when those words leave my mouth. Sometimes I say things that get taken as personal attacks, when that was not my intention at all. But, I have to step back and call out the fact that sometimes I use my words to do the fighting for me. I say something in the heat of the moment that doesn't need to be said. And sometimes that can hurt the people I care about.

Apologizing is something that I never loved to do in the past. Apologizing is basically admitting you may have done something wrong and saying that you wish you hadn't done it. You regret something you said or did. You feel bad about that something and feel the need to say something to make it better. Apologies require you to call out your own sh*t and acknowledge that you did something wrong. That's an uncomfortable thing for a LOT of people to do.

I had to get to a place where I could call out my own sh*t, take ownership for the things I had said or done, and give a damn apology from the heart when necessary. I've gotten to that place now, but it took me years to get here. In the past, I would have been like, "How dare they say that I did something wrong!?" *gasp* It took me growing up and realizing that I just had to own up to the things I said or did to make things get better. I had to call myself out and say,

"Hey! YOU DID THIS. Now do something to fix it."

I think some people just gain this ability with maturity, time, and growth. And therapy doesn't hurt either. I am now able to look at a conflict or situation and see all sides of it. I'm able to remove my personal emotions and be Switzerland in the middle of something and see where maybe I was a cause of some of it as well. I know for some women this is like pulling teeth, and it used to be that way for me too. But if you can call yourself out on your own part in things, it's a whole lot easier to move beyond them, and in a much healthier way at that.

Being so open, raw, and honest about everything in my life in all of my content, it forced me to embrace all of my sh*t. The pretty sh*t, the ugly sh*t, and the sh*t that would have been much easier to just leave out, hide, and ignore. But if there's one thing I've learned along the way, it's that people connect with REAL people. Sure, they love to see everything going right in your life. They love to see your pretty Instagram photos and all of your personal wins. But guess what? My followers LOVE me because I tell them when I'm not doing great too.

I tell my followers when I'm having a rough time. I've filmed YouTube videos through depression episodes. I've cried in my Instastories after having a rough night sober at a wedding. I've put all of my sh*t out for the world to see. The way it's been able to help people was something that I never saw coming, but it is SO worth it.

I'm very opinionated. I'm very outspoken. I was an alcoholic. I was not respectful of myself and my body in the past. Sometimes I say things before I think about them. Sometimes I'm selfish. Sometimes I'm only concerned with what's best for me, and I don't care about anything else. I think that sometimes I should just get my way no matter what's going on. Sometimes I get a little petty. I have a little bit of trust issues that creep back out from time to time. Sometimes I get more emotional about things than I should. Sometimes I'm just a bitch abut things…

I can call out all of these things about myself, and I could call out a lot more if I kept going. The older I get, the more I'm able to do this. To acknowledge and call out all of my sh*t about who I am and what I do.

I'm owning the fact that I'm not perfect. Because nobody is. I have my own issues, my own problems, and my own things that I'd like to continue working on and getting better at. Being able to recognize and call out what those things are just took some time for me. It might take time for you too, but you'll get there.

As I mentioned earlier, with growth and maturity I got to this place. Let me tell you, it's a beautiful f*cking place to get to. It's a place where I can stand up and tell myself, "Hey, get your sh*t together…" or, "That wasn't your brightest moment in life." Feeling no hesitation on being able to call myself out is empowering. It's as REAL as it gets. It's me recognizing that I've got a ton of sh*t in my life that I wanna work at and improve on. And that's a good thing. Plain and simple.

It takes a lot of putting your pride aside to call yourself out in life. It's not for the weak of heart. We become so prideful sometimes that the thought of calling out something we did that wasn't good is super difficult. I'm not downplaying it one bit. There's still times that I have to call myself out for something that I did or said that it kills me to do it. I don't want to say that I was wrong. I don't want to admit that maybe I screwed something up myself. But being able to call it out and take ownership for it, is an absolute game changer. I've seen that now over and over again.

I've learned over these past thirty years that we need to be able to call out ourselves in life, for both the good and the bad. We are not perfect and we don't always do things right. We need to call ourselves out for the things we say and do, especially when they are not good things. We need to be able to tell ourselves that we did something wrong. We need to be able to man up and admit to our faults. We must gain the ability to do these things if we ever want to live a healthy life with healthy relationships.

I have to come down off of my soapbox and my pedestal and

realize that I'm not always perfect and I don't always do it all right. I have to call myself out like a champ. It took a while, but I've finally gotten there. And it's made things hella easier in my life. It's made some parts of life a cake walk now compared to how they used to be. Because I am just calling myself out on all of my sh*t now. The sh*t I want to do better. The sh*t I want to do less of. The sh*t I want to mature and grow beyond in life. Try it sometime. Call yourself out on your own sh*t. I dare you.

THING #28 | YOU'VE GOT TO OWN WHO YOU ARE

One day early on during my third year living sober, I walked into my job at the Brow Bar I still work at one day a week. I'm basically self-employed, but I still keep this job one day a week because I just genuinely enjoy it. I enjoy the people, my clients, and the beauty industry as a whole. When I walked into the back room of the store that day, I saw our District Manager sitting at a table with a man I didn't recognize. I assumed she was training him or something and went to put my belongings in my locker before punching in to work. She turned around and saw me and greeted me quickly and went on to introduce me to the gentleman she was training to be a new Manager as well. She introduced me as the "Benefit Brow girl who is our in-house resident YouTuber, author…" and so on, and so on. Initially I was like "Damn okay, just introduce me like a podcast intro highlighting all my accomplishments." *hair flip emoji* I mean, I wasn't complaining. It's nice to hear someone acknowledge all of the things you do!

I said hello and that it was nice to meet him and shook his hand.

Then the questions followed…I've gotten used to this by now.

When people hear the word "author" they often immediately ask what you've written out of pure curiosity. Totally understandable. It's not every day you meet an "author" wearing a bright pink apron, with perfectly waved ombre hair, and her face highlighted to the heavens about to go wax eyebrows for seven hours straight in a retail store. I can't blame him for wondering what I wrote, because often times I question if I look like the typical "author" you would picture in your head. To be honest, I'm still not 100% comfortable with introducing myself using the word "author" because it still feels surreal to me sometimes. But I'm getting there!

Anyway, of course he asked what it was I had written. I paused for a moment and a lot of thoughts rushed through my brain all at once. Should I tell someone at my corporate job that I had struggled with alcoholism? Should I tell this man in front of my own district manager that I used to have zero control over my drinking? Would he judge me? Would he immediately have a predisposed attitude towards me? Would she change her view of me even though I've worked here for five years and have never even gotten written up? Would they stereotype me as an "addict" in a negative way? It was like a tornado of thoughts went through my head in a span of about three seconds.

In the past I wouldn't have wanted to share the truth about my story with someone so quickly, but that has changed for me over the years. In the past I might have just said "Oh, some personal development type books…" and just brushed the conversation off and tried to leave the situation as quickly as possible. But this time, I chose to f*cking OWN IT.

I looked at him, smiled brightly, and said, "Yes! I wrote a memoir about my sobriety. I just celebrated three years of sobriety a few months ago." BOOM. MIC. F*CKING. DROP. There it was. It was the most empowering moment that I hadn't even seen coming. I wasn't scared, ashamed, or fearful…I didn't hide any part of who I was or what I have been through. I owned it. I owned the sh*t out of it. I owned who I was. I owned my story. It felt f*cking AMAZING.

His response? "Wow. That's incredible. Congratulations!" He smiled and looked at me in a warm and encouraging way. Maybe he did judge me a little bit somewhere inside, but I couldn't see it if he did. See? That wasn't so hard. Why was I so worried about how to respond? Why was I so apprehensive to just own my story?

I realized that I had been worried about something that wasn't even happening. I had assumed that this man would judge me. I had assumed that I would be better off hiding that part of who I was to avoid stereotypes and being seen as someone less than who I really was. The truth was, telling him the truth didn't do any of those things. I felt absolutely fine. In fact, I felt awesome.

There have been many times in my life the past several years that I have hidden things about myself and my story. I have hidden these things out of shame, fear, and guilt. I have hidden things about myself at the chance that people might see me differently. I have shrunk things about myself and who I am as to not stir the pot. I've watered down my story to be safe. I've let myself become small to avoid the attention being focused on my struggles in life. It's not uncommon. Not one bit. A lot of us do this.

Many of us, as women, feel the need to not show our flaws. We don't want to tell people about how we have struggled or had problems. We like to show the highlight reel and all the good things about ourselves.

Why do we do this? Fear. Shame. Guilt. Fear of judgement. Shame for struggling. Guilt about our past "mistakes". Fear that someone will look at us differently. Shame that our lives didn't go as perfectly as we wanted them to or thought they should go. Guilt about the fact that we had to hit a rock bottom to be able to change our lives.

If you follow me on any social media or have read any of my other content, then you already know that I bulldozed through this one a while ago. I chose at some point to own everything about myself, my story, and who I am.

That was a CHOICE. I could have stayed hidden and small. I could have not let the world know about the things I've been through. I could have kept all these things locked away in a dark little box somewhere and kept them my personal secrets. But I chose not to for a reason that was bigger than myself.

I've been able to build an amazing career where I can actually help people. I can change lives. By choosing to own who I am, incredible amazing things have happened. By being my most raw, honest, authentic, vulnerable version of myself, I've been able to move mountains. I've been able to inspire people to change their own lives. I've been able to show people that life in sobriety can be a beautiful and amazing thing. I've shown women that we have a choice and that we have power over who we want to be in life.

All of that became possible because I owned who I was. I showed others that they could do exactly the same thing in their own lives, too. It became something that has been truly beautiful to watch in myself and in others.

If I had hidden part of who I am, none of this would have been possible. If I had hidden my story and not owned all of it, I wouldn't be here right now. You wouldn't be reading this. I'd be stuck struggling and hiding things about my life. I'd be unhappy. I'd feel ashamed. I'd feel less than. I wouldn't have this sense of pride, confidence, and gratitude that I feel day in and day out.

I have learned just how powerful it can be to own the f*ck out of who you are. I have never felt so alive and in acceptance of my entire life as I do now. I have never been so proud. I have never felt this confident in myself before.

Getting to a place where I have been able to accept and own every bit and piece of who I am is one of the greatest feelings in life. How amazing is it to think that we can get to this place on our own? We can absolutely feel every bit of this by choosing to simply stand up for and own everything about who we are as a person.

I was (and will always be deep down) an alcoholic. That has been the biggest and the hardest one for me to own, hands down. I can remember when I first started online dating while sober that I never wanted to share my story about why I was sober. The guy would ask over dinner, "So, why don't you drink?" and I would always respond with a short response along the lines of, "Oh, it's a long story..." and never actually tell the story. I was scared that the guy would judge me and never want to see me again. I was hiding a part of who I was to avoid judgement and rejection. I was terrified of what they would think if they knew the truth about my past.

It took a while, and a lot of awkward first dates dodging that question, but I finally got to a point where I included my sobriety right smack dab in the front of my dating app bio. I included that I was the author of a book called *Sober As F**** right there for them to see before they decided whether to swipe right or left on me. I even had a photo of myself holding my book from my first speaking event as one of my main photos at one point. And guess what happened... I got message after message saying how awesome it was that I was sober. I got message after message saying how impressive it was that I had written and self-published a book. I even had a random guy I never met send me a message that he had ordered my book just to show support because he thought what I was doing was amazing. Again, why had I been so worried about just owning my story and who I was? There was nothing to be afraid of, and everything to be proud of.

For the first two years of my sobriety, I struggled to say the word alcoholic when I spoke about myself. It was easier to me to say I had a, "problem with alcohol" then to actually say that word out loud. I didn't want to admit it. I didn't want to accept that term as defining who I was. I had to ask myself why? Why was it such a bad thing for me to just own it? What was I gaining by not accepting it for myself? Nothing. I was just hiding myself and who I was. I was hiding the things that made me who I am and got me to where I am today.

The first time I felt like I truly owned my whole story and everything about who I am was when I self-published *Sober As F****. It was like I had finally let it all go out into the world. I had put it out there for everyone to see. I had owned every bit of my past and my struggles with alcohol. I owned every bit of my recovery and sobriety. It was like I put out that book and said "THIS IS ME. TAKE IT OR LEAVE IT..." I stopped giving a f*** about what others might think. I owned the hell out of it, and it was one of the biggest days of my entire life.

What I've learned is that we cannot be ashamed of the things that have shaped us into who we are today. We cannot avoid owning who we are because of things like fear, shame, and guilt.

We need to own who we are with pride, grace, and love instead. We need to take every bit and piece of who we are with confidence and with our head held high. Never shrink. Never water anything down. Never make yourself small. Never be quiet. Never hide. Own every little thing about yourself and who you are. Own it. OWN the sh*t out of ALL of it.

THING #29 | EVERY MINUTE, EVERY CHOICE, & EVERY LITTLE PUZZLE PIECE IS PART OF A MUCH BIGGER PICTURE

Have you ever stopped at any given moment during any given day and really thought about how things come together in our lives? Have you ever thought about a string of events and wondered what would have happened if one thing had happened differently? How if we made one small choice differently how it could have changed and derailed everything that would happen as a result of it? Think about how one little choice could have changed the entire game plan of your life. This is some pretty high level, woo-woo sh*t...I know. But if you can really try to get outside of your own practical mind and think about this, it can absolutely BLOW your mind.

Over time I have realized that every single thing in my life has been a puzzle piece to a much bigger picture. That even the smallest little things have caused a chain reaction to make everything else happen exactly as it has. It's mind boggling to think about it really... That every choice we make every minute of every single day has the power to change the direction and the outcome of our entire life.

Even the tiniest change in the course of our life could set off a whole other life to play out. It's kind of like a domino effect if you really think about. What it you hadn't walked into that bar on that night where you met the love of your life? What if you got stuck in traffic and missed that job interview? What if something happened that put that one domino out of place, setting off a whole other chain of dominos to fall instead?

Is your mind absolutely blown by this idea yet? Because sometimes when I think back to how things could have gone differently and turned into a whole different life right now my mind could absolutely explode at the thought of it all. Sometimes I will look back and think about if one thing had gone differently, what would my life look like right now? How different would it be?

The one that always throws me for a loop and makes me feel a million different emotions deals with the night I got sober...What if I hadn't made it? What if that night in the Emergency Room my body didn't pull through? What if I hadn't gotten to the hospital in time? What if someone put me in my car to "sleep it off" and I ended up dead? There are a million different scenarios that I've run through in my head over and over again for the past few years. Honestly, I could drive myself crazy if I kept thinking of how bad it could have ended up.

Sometimes I question what would have happened if that night hadn't happened at all. Sometimes I question how things could have gone differently. What if I hadn't had that much alcohol? What if I hadn't taken all of those pills? What if I hadn't gone to that music festival? There's a chance I would have never gotten sober. There's a chance I wouldn't be who I am now. There's a chance I would have still been abusing alcohol on a regular basis. I could have been a full blown alcoholic drinking on a daily basis. So many things could have happened as a result of that night not happening. It could have set off a completely different life for me.

I could replay that night a million different times and in a million different ways. Ninety-nine percent of the possible ways it could have gone involve me being dead. I don't say this to be morbid, I say it to be realistic. I could very well not be here right now. I could have already been gone for years. My mother could have buried her daughter just after her twenty-sixth birthday. That is the absolute truth about what happened. But what I have to remind myself is that it happened exactly as it was meant to happen. And it happened this way for a reason.

That night was not meant to be the end of the road for me. God, angels, the Universe, and whatever other Higher Powers there are out there decided that there was more for me in life than to die that night. That night was just the result of one choice, one minute, and one part of my puzzle coming together exactly as it was supposed to. There was a much bigger picture for my life beyond what I could even fathom, and every little thing that happened was putting the picture together.

It's easy to fall into the trap of the "what ifs" when it comes to all areas of our lives. We will question over and over again how things may have been different if we had chosen to do one little thing differently. We might daydream about how things would have played out if we had made a different choice. What if we stayed with the guy? What if we went away to college? What if we had chased that crazy dream? What if we missed that flight? We can create an entire alternate world in our head if we get too crazy about overanalyzing and questioning "But what if I had done this instead..."

I now realize that every thing that has happened along the way has been a literal domino effect. Every single choice and every single moment of every single day of my past has led directly to the next thing and so on and so on.

I learned that I can go back and rethink every minute, every choice, every little piece of the puzzle over and over again and drive myself insane trying to understand the meaning of it all. The meaning of it all is bigger than anything I will ever understand while I'm in the middle of it. There is a purpose and a plan laid out for my life that has been there all along. It's one big journey that is meant for me to live out. I don't know exactly where it's going to take me or what's going to happen next, but I know it's going to take me to wherever it is I'm meant to be. I have faith in that.

There is a much bigger picture for all of us in life. There is a plan and a purpose and a place that we are meant to get to. Most of the time we will never be able to see it before we get there. We won't be able to figure it out before we are meant to. No matter how hard we try, we won't be able to see our destiny until it is time. Our life will be like a scavenger hunt where we are constantly moving towards our ultimate purpose and bigger picture.

It will all come together one day and every little piece along the way will make complete and total sense. Our disappointments will make sense. Our heartbreaks will have a purpose. We will see what every success in our life was leading towards. We will finally be able to make sense of the things that were never clear before.

We will have this type of awakening one day where all of the pieces will come together. The bigger picture will finally start to make sense. Every choice, every minute, every piece of the puzzle will finally come together.

The bigger picture for my life was getting to where I am today… Alive, happy, healthy, and sharing my story to help others. THIS was the big picture and purpose of my life. This is exactly what I was meant to get to and this is who I was meant to become. I realize now looking back that every single little thing along the way got me here.

Every choice got me here. Every mistake got me here. Every little thing was just a stepping stone towards my purpose. Each thing was just one single domino in a line of hundreds of other dominos that would fall one after the other automatically. Everything in my life has set off a chain reaction of other things to be right here, right now… sharing this with all of you.

It's a complex thing to realize, but this is exactly how all of our lives happen. We have no control over it at all. It's our destiny. We do one thing, we make one choice, and it sets off everything that will happen afterwards as a result.

This is how life gets us to where we are meant to go. This is how we get to and discover our destiny. This is how we see what the bigger picture is for our life, and see how every little thing along the way lined up perfectly to get us there. Crazy, isn't it?

I've learned to let go and let life happen. I've learned that I will always get to that big picture that is destined for my life. Is it where I am today? Right now, yes. Is there a whole other chain of events waiting for me in my future that will take me to a completely different place that I'm not even aware of yet? Probably. All I know is that I will continue living in the moment and knowing that every little thing that happens will happen exactly as it should to get me to exactly where I am supposed to be.

Let go. Have faith. Trust the process. Live this life in the moment. Enjoy the journey. Try to wrap your head around this idea that every minute, every choice, and every little puzzle piece in your life is a part of your bigger picture. You're going exactly where you're supposed to go. You're being led to exactly where you are supposed to be. You're being carefully built and shaped into who you are meant to become.

Choosing to buy and read this book was not only one little piece of the puzzle of your life, but also a part of mine. So, thank you for being one of the little pieces of my puzzle. Each and every one of you make up one of them. Thank you for being one of those dominos that has lined up in my life.

THING #30 | YOU CAN CHOOSE TO MAKE YOUR LIFE YOUR BEST F*CKING LIFE

Now if you follow me at all anywhere on the internet or have spent a few minutes around me in real life, you knew this one was coming. You know that your girl here is THE biggest advocate for all things female empowerment, self love, self care, dating yourself, and living your best life possible every single day of your life. My podcast is literally called *Her Best F***ing Life* because I am so passionate about and completely OBSESSED with this idea. I live every single day of my life making sure that it is the best that it can be. Over the top. Unnecessarily good. Extra. I'm talking about doing things everyday and saying "just living my best life" and not feeling one bit bad about it. #sorrynotsorry

Call it selfish. Call it narcissistic. But, you know what? I'm over here living my best f*cking life because of it. And what I need to tell you right here, right now is that YOU have every right to be doing it too.

I learned that it was nobody's responsibility but my own to make my life my best f*cking life possible. Nobody else was gonna do it for me, I had to make the choice to make it happen for myself. I'm gonna tell you all about how I started doing this, what happened when I started doing this, and why it's so important for you to do this too. Ready? Let's go.

I got this big idea after I got sober and after I got my heart broken. I decided to be alone and really figure my sh*t out. I was going to really do the self work. Everything was going to be great. It was going to be this amazing spiritual journey where I discovered myself like every female lead role does in chick flicks after everything in her life falls apart. It sounded pretty cut and dry. I was going to have my Elle Woods moment after Warner left her in *Legally Blonde*. I was going to go to Harvard Law. Okay, I'm obviously f*cking joking, per usual. But you catch my drift.

What actually happened when I did this? I got lonely as hell. I didn't go out much. I felt like such a loner. I started to get regular episodes of depression. I lost some of my "friends." My anxiety went crazy. My life was definitely not my best life. I was not in a good place emotionally, mentally, or physically. Honestly, it was not the prettiest time in my life...until I finally woke up and did something about it.

Something had to shift. Something had to change. I couldn't keep sitting around wondering why I wasn't living the life I envisioned in my head. I saw so many women out there living lives that they loved, and I wanted that for my own life too I wanted my life to feel as genuinely happy and as full of positivity as possible. I wanted to feel like my life was pleasant and enjoyable every single day. I wanted to smile and feel grateful every single day. I wanted my life to be everything I dreamed it could be and more...my BEST life.

I decided that I didn't like the way things were going. I didn't want to feel sad anymore. I didn't want to only look forward to certain days of the week. I didn't want to feel like I needed a man just to be complete. I didn't want to constantly feel like there was always something more that would make me happier. I wanted to genuinely enjoy every single day of my life. I wanted every day of my life to be the best day of my life.

It sounded a little crazy and little bit like something a guy that looked like he had five sister wives back home would be telling you on an infomercial when you woke up at 4 a.m. after leaving the TV on. But, was it really so crazy to think that it was possible?

So, I chose to change my life. I decided to change everything about the way I was living. I went on a relentless journey to create my best f*cking life. I was going to do all the self care. I was going to go on the trips I wanted to take. I was going to do all the special extra things for myself. I was going to fall in love with myself. I was going to look at every single day and figure out how I could make it just a little bit better. I was going to be selfish as f*ck about creating the best life I possibly could day in and day out. It was like my own personal female empowerment movement with myself. And I dove head first right into it.

I started to look at every day, every situation, every thing I did and ask myself, "How could I make this a little bit better?" or, "What would make me enjoy this just a little bit more?" I would stop and say in my head, "What would make this feel more special?" It felt a little vain at first, but it also felt really, really good. This is how the whole idea of "baby life upgrades" started.

If you follow me on social media or listen to my podcast, then you already know! If you don't...allow me to break it down for you. This one is VERY simple to do. Look at whatever you are doing and ask yourself how you could make it better. Ask yourself how you could make it a little bit more enjoyable. Ask yourself how you could make it a little more "extra."

Baby life upgrades are exactly what they sound like: small, easy to make changes that make you feel special. They make you feel a little bit more elevated. They are a little bit of an upgrade from the norm. They are the ultimate justification for living by the motto of "treat yoself."

The next thing I started to do was to date myself. I've covered this topic in podcasts, books, and all over my social media as well. I know this one can feel a little bit silly and uncomfortable for a lot of people at first. I'll admit that it felt awkward as hell to me at first. What am I, an asexual now? I was THAT single that I had to start dating myself? Guess I should buy a pair of hot pink bedazzled Crocs and adopt eight cats while I'm at it too.

Dating yourself does not need to be this weird, awkward thing. And attention to all my dating and married women out there, you DON'T have to be single to do it! I simply started thinking about the things I would be doing with my significant other if I had one. What would we go do as dates? Would they make me dinner? Would they take me to the movies? Would they buy me flowers? Would we take a quick weekend getaway together? I asked myself all these question and then asked myself the most important question... "Why can't I do these things for my damn myself?"

This was how my concept of dating yourself started. I thought of all the things I wasn't doing just because I didn't have a significant other and asked myself why the hell I couldn't do these things if I was single?

Did I not deserve special evenings? Did I not deserve a home-cooked meal? Was I not supposed to go on weekend getaways because I didn't have a man? HELL NO. It was finally like a wake up call to myself. I deserved all the things, and I could do them all for my damn self. One vase of gorgeous white roses at a time.

I also started saying "YES" to the things that I wanted to do relentlessly. The things that made me happy. The things that I enjoyed. The extra things. The unnecessary things. The whipped cream on my latte. The pedicure in the middle of winter when nobody was seeing my feet. The new desk for my office in our new house when my old desk was still working just fine. YES, PLEASE!

I stopped second guessing if things that would make me happy were necessary, a waste of money, or if I would survive in life just fine without them. It didn't matter. If they made that particular day of my life feel a little bit happier, a little bit brighter, and a little bit more special...well then sign me up!

I started giving myself permission. Permission to be who I wanted to be. Permission to do what I wanted to do. Permission to dream as big as I wanted to dream. I decided that I didn't need anyone's permission but my own when it came to how I wanted to live each day of my live. And then I learned that I had never needed anyone's permission all along. It was always on me.

I was the one holding myself back. I was the one not doing the things to make myself happy. I was the one not making my days as full of happiness as they could have been all along. I was the one saying I needed someone else to complete me. I was the one telling myself the extra things weren't necessary. I was the one withholding the permission to do all of the things I wanted to do.

When I realized that I held all of the power and energy within myself to create my best life possible all along…it was like my whole world changed.

I started sharing the way I was living on social media through my blog, my YouTube channel, my podcast episodes, my books, my Instagram stories, and just about anywhere else you could think of. What happened after I started doing this made the whole thing really catch fire…other women wanted this for their own lives. And suddenly, I had a platform to tell them that they had the power to do it too.

Ladies, I'm gonna preach like a Christian on Sunday morning here for a minute, so brace yourselves. I'm about to get you all kinds of fired up. I'm about to light a fire under your *ss and inside of your heart that will inspire you to make some major moves. Y'all ready for this?

The only reason you are not living your best f*cking life is because you haven't chosen to. You haven't made the choice. You haven't taken the steps. You haven't made the changes. You haven't stepped up and said, "THIS IS THE LIFE I WANT FOR MYSELF."

That ends today. Unless you want to stay stuck and keep living small. Unless you are okay with being complacent in your life. It ends today. It's time to move. It's time to make changes. It's time to make shifts. Shifts that will change every day of your life into one that is better. One that is happier. One that is brighter. One that is your best f*cking life.

What I learned by the time my twenties were over is that if I want to live my best f*cking life, then it was all on me. I could have started living this way at any point had I just made that choice.

Now that I realized that I always had and always will have that power, there is nobody to blame but myself if I'm not living in the way that I want to. I learned just how much influence I have over myself, my mindset, my mood, my actions, my emotions, and everything else in my life.

I learned that I could give myself as much self love and self care as I needed on any given day. Did I need a break for a bubble bath and a face mask? Then I was going to make sure I took that time at the end of my day. Did I need to just relax and recharge? Then I was going to make sure I did that. Did I need to do something special for myself on a day that was just feeling "blah?" Then I was going to choose to do something for myself.

We, as women, tend to not put ourselves first. We put the needs of others above our own. It's time we put ourselves back up at the top with everyone else. Because if we want to start living our best life, it's going to require us to start prioritizing ourselves again, too.

This is a battle cry to all of the women out there not choosing to make their life their best one possible. You deserve it. It is necessary. Give yourself the love and care you so freely hand out to others. Think of yourself and what you need right here, right now. And start making changes in your life to reflect the life that you desire to live.

We have the power to make each and every day of our lives into exactly what we want it to be. We have the opportunity to make sure that we treat ourselves well. We have the right to put ourselves first when necessary. We have the right to do special things for ourselves simply because we can. We have every damn right to live our best f*cking life every day of our life, and it's about time we stand up and choose to start doing exactly that. We are in the driver's seat when it comes to what we want our lives to be. Girl, it's time you take back the f*cking wheel.

EPILOGUE

Thirty as F***... Here we are. I can honestly say that this has been one of the most enjoyable subjects I've written about so far. The serious and deep books about my sobriety are some of the most meaningful and fulfilling things I've ever created in my life, no doubt. They were what started my whole career with writing. But, this book was different. This book was my chance to lighten up. This book was my chance to laugh. This book was my chance to breathe. This book was my chance to show yet another side of who I am and what I have to offer to the world with my voice and my story.

After starting my podcast, *Her Best F***ing Life*, I realized that I had more to talk about than just sobriety. Sobriety will definitely always be my biggest passion and the closest thing to my heart. There is nothing I love more than knowing my story about getting and living sober has been able to help and inspire others. Knowing that my story has given them hope to change their own life is the most humbling thing that I could ever ask for in life. I will forever be grateful for it all. But I wanted to switch things up with my next book that I would write.

Once I started talking about all areas of life on my podcast episodes, people were here for it. You guys were loving every minute of it. I received so many messages, emails, and comments about my podcast episodes from women all over the world. My inbox was flooded with, "OMG, THIS SPOKE TO ME," or, "This is exactly what I needed to hear today!" over and over again.

Hearing these responses inspired me to share more. It left me wanting to give you more of this authentic and raw woman you guys have grown to know and love. It's so freeing and empowering knowing that I can be every bit of myself and connect with women all over the world, all while swearing like a sailor and not getting criticized about it one bit.

You guys have let me be ME to the truest extent. You've supported me and rallied around me with every little thing I've done. You've bought the books, listened to the podcasts, bought the merch, did the coaching, watched the YouTube videos and so on and so on.

I have never felt so supported and appreciated for just being myself and being honest. I have never felt so supported and loved by people that I've never even met. Some of you guys are absolute strangers to me and have shown up for me again and again, sometimes more than my own friends and family have. That is what inspired me to write this book next…knowing that you incredible women would be here with your support just like you have been all along.

I wanted to share with you all how f*cked up this time in our lives can be. I wanted to bring you into my twisted little head full of curse words, brutal honesty, and hilarious realizations about my young adult life. I wanted to take the non-sugarcoated attitude of my podcast and turn it into an entire book for you to dive into. I wanted you to curl up in bed with *Thirty As F**** and laugh your asses off at how absolutely ridiculous we females can be at times. I also wanted to leave you guys with some real takeaways that you could apply to your own life to make it even better. After all, we're all out here just trying to live our best f*cking life, right ladies?

This book has been so different for me in more ways than one.

I've come into this book not feeling as uncertain or insecure about myself as I have with my past books. This book was the first time I finally felt comfortable referring to myself as an "author." This book was the first time I didn't feel pressured like a crazy person to make it "perfect" and something that everyone would like. It was the first time I was confident that I was going to write a bad*ss book, without a doubt.

This book was the first time I felt legit enough to share with someone that just maybe I would consider putting myself on the cover. That maybe I would put myself on the front of my book just like the real, successful authors out there do...because I am one of those people too. I may not be rich and famous, but to me THIS is being a real, successful author. Pouring myself into this book and having amazing people out there in the world finding it, reading it, and sharing it. So your girl is on the cover, smiling bright as hell.

I have so much heart and soul that I've poured into *Thirty as F****. I feel like I've owned every little bit of my sh*t and who I am in this one. I'm standing tall and proud of this one. I hope it made you laugh. I hope it made you smile. I hope it made you cry, but only good tears. Good tears because you realize that you are not alone in this journey of life as a woman. I'm here with you ladies every step of the way. I hope that you guys have enjoyed reading this one just as much as I enjoyed writing it for you. xx.

BIG THANKS

To the person or people I always end up forgetting to thank, thank you.

Thank you to God, the Universe, and whatever Higher Powers are always out there steering me through this crazy journey called life. It's crazy sometimes how much I can trust that you are all working to take me to where I am meant to be. It's insane to notice the signs and redirection you place in my way. Thank you for finally making me be a "woo-woo" woman who can open her heart to things bigger than herself.

Andrew. You are the fuel to my crazy fire that burns inside. You make sure that I never think any dream or goal is too far away. You inspire me to live big and love big. Thank you for being a part of this amazing life I get to live. Thank you for making my dreams come true. Thank you for giving me my best f*cking life every single day of my life.

My online girl gang... YOU LADIES. You are the reason this all happens. You are the ones buying the books, listening to the podcast episodes, and always showing the most love. Sometimes you guys show up more than the people I am closest with in my life do. It's always mind-blowing to me how much complete strangers on the internet can have your back so much and love you so big. Don't think for a second that I am not grateful and SO appreciative for all of it. This is all because of you. SO MUCH LOVE.

Thank you to my amazing circle of friends. You ladies inspire me again and again to show up and make magic happen. Thank you for sticking around through the Hot Mess Express phase, the Sobriety phase, and all the other phases along the way. Thank you for showing me what real friendship looks like regardless of miles, years, life changes, and anything else that might try to get in the way.

Thank you to my family for teaching me and showing me so much in life. Thank you for making me who I am today. Especially you, Mom. You will forever be my biggest critic but also my biggest supporter. Thank you for always allowing me to push boundaries and test waters growing up, and for always being my best friend. Love you lots.

Thank you to my therapist, Debbie. You have walked me through lots of tears, lots of smiles, and more growth than I could have ever done alone. Through heartbreaks, sobriety, big changes, and everything… Thank you.

The behind the scenes magic makers! Thank you to Jason & Emma of Collective Image Photography. Thank you for making my cover vision truly come to life! Thank for for also letting me dance to "Africa" while doing it. Thank you to Cara Lockwood for always being an amazing and encouraging editor. Thank you to Caroline Teagle for making one amazing cover after another and dealing with my one million tweaks and changes!

A big, HUGE thank you to every single one of you that bought this book. This was my fifth piece I released and you guys never fail to show up every single time in support! Thank you for being a part of my magic. xx .

ABOUT THE AUTHOR

As an entrepreneur, makeup artist, self-publisher author, YouTuber, mindset coach, podcast host, and blogger, Sarah Ordo is your not-so-average Millennial craving to leave her mark on this world in more ways than one.

Sarah's award-winning on location hair and makeup company (based out of Detroit), 24Luxe Hair & Makeup, has been styling women for their special events since 2013. Her social media pages reach thousands of followers daily featuring a variety of beauty, health, lifestyle, sobriety, and wellness posts. Her YouTube videos documenting and following her sobriety have reached millions of viewers internationally, and have even been featured on *Dateline NBC*. Sarah has been featured on and interviewed for numerous blogs and podcasts including Cara Alwill Leyba's *Style Your Mind* Podcast and Courtney Bentley's *Fit Fierce & Fabulous* Podcast.

On her podcast *Her Best F***ing Life*, Sarah loves to talk about all topics surrounding how to create a life you love, your best life possible. The episodes feature a no-bullsh*t approach to life, amazing guest interviews, and a whole lot of swearing. On her website, *sarahordo.com,* Sarah blogs about living sober, self-love, mental health, and many other raw, honest topics. She also sells merchandise on her website for her books and podcast.

*Sober as F*** was the first full-length memoir and book written by Sarah, released in May 2017. She has gone on to publish *Innerbloom, Sober As F***:The Workbook*, and the *Her Best F***ing Life Planner,* which are all available on Amazon & Kindle.

Connect with Sarah:
www.sarahordo.com
Youtube: Sarah Ordo
Instagram: @24Luxe_Sarah
Podcast: Her Best F***ing Life (on iTunes & Stitcher)
Books: Amazon & Kindle

Made in the USA
Middletown, DE
11 February 2022

60969886R00137